REVISE EDEXCEL GCSE
ICT

D0184154

REVISION WORKBOOK

Series Consultant: Harry Smith   Authors: Nicola Hughes and David Waller

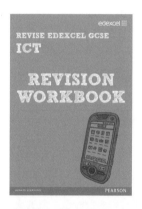

THE REVISE EDEXCEL SERIES
Available in print or online

Online editions for all titles in the Revise Edexcel series are available Autumn 2012.

Presented on our ActiveLearn platform, you can view the full book and customise it by adding notes, comments and weblinks.

Print editions

ICT Revision Workbook	9781446903896
ICT Revision Guide	9781446903872

Online editions

ICT Revision Workbook	9781446903841
ICT Revision Guide	9781446903834

This Revision Workbook is designed to complement your classroom and home learning, and to help prepare you for the exam. It does not include all the content and skills needed for the complete course. It is designed to work in combination with Edexcel's main GCSE ICT 2010 series.

To find out more visit:
www.pearsonschools.co.uk/edexcelgcseICTrevision

ALWAYS LEARNING   **PEARSON**

Contents

A small bit of small print

Edexcel publishes Sample Assessment Material, the Specification and Technology Update on its website. This is the official content and this book should be used in conjunction with it. The questions in this book have been written to help you practise what you have learned in your revision. Remember: the real exam questions may not look like this.

Target grades

Target grades are quoted in this book for some of the questions. Students targeting this grade should be aiming to get some of the marks available. Students targeting a higher grade should be aiming to get all of the marks available.

Uses of digital devices

C–B

(a) Explain **one** way in which the use of digital devices has improved the way in which companies work and operate. **(2 marks)**

> **Guided**

EXAM ALERT

The use of video conferencing means that ...people... can communicate at any time, wherever they are.

Students have struggled with exam questions similar to this – **be prepared!** ResultsPlus

C–A*

(b) *Discuss the benefits of the use of personal digital devices in education. **(6 marks)**

This question has an asterisk which means that the quality of your written communication will be assessed. You need to think about your spelling, punctuation and grammar as well as clarity of expression. You should make a list of all the points you want to make and then plan out your answer before you start writing. Think about the following points:
- the personal digital devices that can be used in education
- the use of specialist software
- the use of personal digital devices for communicating.

teens can use it for homework to find info. They can use software like word.
work on the go
work at any time
Devices such as : * laptops
                  * tablets
                  * smartphones
can all be used by students for educational put purposes i.e to use BBC Bitesize

Had a go ☐　Nearly there ☐　Nailed it! ☐

Using digital devices

*The use of digital devices has had a huge impact on people and society but some people have limited access to digital technology.

Discuss the impact this has on their lifestyle.

(6 marks)

This question has an asterisk which means that the quality of your written communication will be assessed. You need to think about your spelling, punctuation and grammar as well as clarity of expression. You should make a list of all the points you want to make and then plan out your answer before you start writing. Think about the effects of limited access to digital technology in terms of:
- economic impact
- social impact
- educational impact
- cultural impact.

Students have struggled with exam questions similar to this – **be prepared!**

ResultsPlus

Increases the amount of global warming.
teens can use it for social networking, like skype (VOIP) or ~~fatti~~ video chat, facebook or ~~twitter~~ twitter. People with limited access to internet may find it harder to communicate with friends and family through voip.

Common features

G (a) Study the four digital devices below.

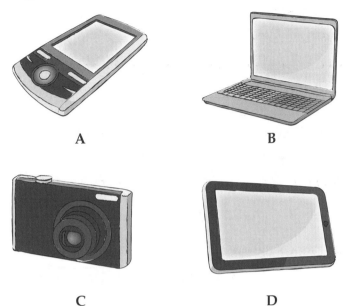

A

B

C

D

Which of the devices shown contains a processor? **(1 mark)**

☐ **A** B only

☐ **B** D only

☐ **C** None of them

☑ **D** All of them

> Remember that a processor controls all functions of a device.

 D-C (b) Some digital devices store data on internal hard disk drives and others use SD cards.

(i) Give two advantages of using a hard disk drive rather than an SD card. **(2 marks)**

Guided

EXAM ALERT

1 A hard disk drive has greater storage capacity.

2 Faster access to data

> Students have struggled with exam questions similar to this – **be prepared!** ResultsPlus

 B-A (ii) Give **two** advantages of using an SD card rather than a hard disk drive. **(2 marks)**

1 SD transfers (reads/writes) data faster is lighter

2 It is more mobile, no moving parts

> Questions 2(a) and 2(b) are comparison questions. Both ask you to compare storing data on hard disk drives and storing data on SD cards. This means you need to think of four differences between the two storage methods in total.

Target Achieved.

Input and output devices

E   (a) Some input and output devices can be either inbuilt or external.

Give **one** reason why an inbuilt webcam might be more convenient than an external one when video conferencing. **(1 mark)**

There is no hassle with wires getting in the way.

D   (b) Ann always uses a headset when video conferencing.

State **one** advantage of using a headset. **(1 mark)**

clearer audio quality

F   (c) This table shows the specifications of three tablet computers.

	Tablet computer A	Tablet computer B	Tablet computer C
Microphone	none	none	internal
Connectivity	USB 2.0, Bluetooth	Bluetooth	Wi-Fi
Storage	8 GB	32 GB	8 GB
Processor speed	600 MHz	1 GHz	800 MHz
SIM card slot	no	yes	no

State which **one** of these tablet computers could be used for VoIP without a peripheral device. **(1 mark)**

C

> VoIP calls are voice calls made over the Internet.

D   (d) Chris uses a laptop for work. The laptop has an inbuilt screen but Chris connects his laptop to a monitor as well.

Give **one** possible reason for this. **(1 mark)**

Higher resolution screen.

> Think about what a monitor offers Chris that his laptop screen cannot.

EXAM ALERT

> Students have struggled with exam questions similar to this – **be prepared!** ResultsPlus

Target Achieved.

Connectivity

Fatima has several digital devices including a laptop computer, smartphone and media player.

F-E

(a) Fatima often connects them together to transfer data between them.

Give **two** wireless connectivity methods that can be used to transfer data between devices. **(2 marks)**

1 _bluetooth_

2 _NFC (Near Field Communication)_

(b) Fatima connects her smartphone and her media player to her laptop to synchronise them.

B-A

(i) Explain what is meant by 'synchronisation'. **(2 marks)**

Keeping multiple files on different devices that are the same. If something is updated on one device, it will be updated across the others.

D-C

(ii) When Fatima connects her media player to her laptop she often sees the dialogue box shown in Figure 1.

Guided

Media Player Software Update

Update in progress...

Cancel

Figure 1

The update includes a security fix for the software.

Give **two other** reasons for a software update. **(2 marks)**

1 To fix or patch bugs.

2 _add tweaks_

C-B

(c) Fatima has been advised that she can use 'cloud storage' with her devices.

Explain why 'cloud storage' is useful when owning multiple devices. **(2 marks)**

If not all files can fit on one device it can be stored in the cloud.

> You are being asked to explain the benefits of synchronising devices using data stored on a remote server on the Internet.

Target Achieved.

Had a go ☐ Nearly there ☐ Nailed it! ☐

Mobile phones 1

	Mobile phone A	Mobile phone B	Mobile phone C	Mobile phone D
Camera	8.1 MP	5 MP	3.2 MP	2 MP
Storage	64 MB	8 GB	128 MB	256 MB
Memory card	SDHC	none	SD	none
Music	MP3 player, FM radio	MP3 player	MP3 player	MP3 player
Video	none	none	none	calling
Email	POP3	IMAP4	POP3	POP3
Connectivity	Wi-Fi, Bluetooth, GPS	Wi-Fi, Bluetooth	Wi-Fi, Bluetooth	Bluetooth
Network band	quad	tri	dual	quad

Use the information in the table above to help you answer the following questions.

Jon wants to buy a new mobile phone.

(G) **(a)** Which one of these mobile phones has the largest storage? **(1 mark)**

☐ Mobile phone A

☒ Mobile phone B

☐ Mobile phone C

☐ Mobile phone D

(F) **(b)** The mobile phone with the highest resolution camera is: **(1 mark)**

☒ Mobile phone A

☐ Mobile phone B

☐ Mobile phone C

☐ Mobile phone D

(F) **(c)** Jon wants to 'surf the web' on his phone.

State **one** feature the phone could have to make this possible. **(1 mark)**

Wi-Fi

(F-E) **(d)** Phone A has GPS as one of its features.

State **two** uses of GPS on a mobile phone. **(2 marks)**

Guided

1   Using a sat nav app on your mobile phone, GPS can help you find your way by giving directions from current location to destination.

2   Geotagging images

ICT DEPT MR GRANT

1 4 NOV 2013

6

Mobile phones 2

E-D (a) Amandeep has a mobile phone and he is concerned about data security.

State **two** ways he can protect the information stored on his phone.   **(2 marks)**

1 Add a password

2 ....

D (b) Different mobile phones use different network bands.

The network band of a mobile phone limits: **(1 mark)**

☐ **A** the speed at which data can be downloaded

☒ **B** the countries in which the phone can be used

☐ **C** the data services the phone supports

☐ **D** the choice of mobile network provider.

(c) Susan's parents have promised to buy her a new mobile phone for her fifteenth birthday. Susan plans to use her new phone mostly for entertainment.   *Movies, music*

F-E (i) List **two** features that the phone might need.   **(2 marks)**

1 High resolution screen

2 Good quality speakers

G-F (ii) Susan's phone can output in high definition (HD).
State the connectivity method she would need to output in HD.   **(1 mark)**

HDMI

G-F (iii) Susan wants to play music from her phone.
State **one** peripheral device she might use.   **(1 mark)**

3.5mm headphones/speakers

D (d) Give **one** health and safety concern of using a mobile phone.   **(1 mark)**

RSI strain injury

ICT DEPT MR GRANT
1 4 NOV 2013

————————

Personal computers 1

The table below shows the specifications of four tablet computers.

	Tablet computer A	Tablet computer B	Tablet computer C	Tablet computer D
Microphone	none	none	none	internal
Connectivity	USB 2.0, Wi-Fi	USB 2.0, Bluetooth	Bluetooth	Wi-Fi
Storage	16 GB	8 GB	32 GB	8 GB
Processor speed	1.2 GHz	600 MHz	1 GHz	800 MHz
Weight	680 g	600 g	220 g	650 g
Size	242 × 190 × 13 mm	230 × 180 × 16 mm	150 × 80 × 10 mm	170 × 220 × 14 mm
SIM card slot	No	No	Yes	No

Use the information in the table to help you answer this question.

(F) (a) Which one of these tablet computers is the most portable? **(1 mark)**

☐ Tablet computer A

☐ Tablet computer B

☒ Tablet computer C

☐ Tablet computer D

(E-D) (b) Tablet computer B has a sensor which detects any movement of the device. The device uses data from the sensor to switch itself off if it is dropped.

Give **two other** ways the device could use data from the sensor. **(2 marks)**

> **Guided**

1 Rotating the screen from landscape to portrait depending on which way you are holding the tablet.

2 gaming

> This question is asking you to think about uses of a tablet that require movement.

(F) (c) Tablet computer C has a SIM card slot.

What type of connectivity could this provide? **(1 mark)**

☐ **A** Infrared

☐ **B** Bluetooth

☒ **C** 3G

☐ **D** WLA

ICT DEPT MR GRANT
14 NOV 2013

(F) (d) Tablet computer A has a high resolution screen.

State what is meant by 'high resolution'. **(1 mark)**

high number of pixels

(E) (e) The tablet computers use a touch screen interface instead of a keyboard and mouse.

Give **one** risk to health from the extended use of a touch screen interface. **(1 mark)**

eye strain, RSI

Personal computers 2

Jamie is going to buy a new PC.

E-C

(a) List **two** features of a PC and state why each is important. **(4 marks)**

Feature 1 .....CPU...

Reason .....Brain of the computer...

....

Feature 2 .....GPU...

Reason .....controls graphics performance.................................

....

F

(b) Designers try to make computer equipment as comfortable to use as possible.

The science of designing user-friendly equipment is called **(1 mark)**

☐ **A** Aesthetics

☐ **B** Intelligent design

☒ **C** Ergonomics

☐ **D** Functional design

F

(c) Jamie plays online games all day and gets back pain.

Give **one** cause of this discomfort when using computer equipment. **(1 mark)**

.....Not in correct upright position..

....

E-D

(d) Give **two other** possible health risks when using a computer for long periods and, for each one, suggest a possible solution. **(4 marks)**

> **Guided**

Risk 1 Eye strain from looking at a screen for too long or light falling on the monitor.

Solution .....take breaks..

....

Risk 2 Repetitive strain injury from repeated movements.

Solution .....Take regular brakes..

....

ICT DEPT MR GRANT

14 NOV 2013

_____

Had a go ☐   Nearly there ☐   Nailed it! ☐

Cameras and camcorders 1

The table below shows the specifications of four camcorders.

	Camcorder A	Camcorder B	Camcorder C	Camcorder D
Video format	SD	SD	HD 720p	HD 1080p
Optical zoom	none	none	15×	12×
Digital zoom	none	2×	18×	30×
LCD screen	none	2″ colour	3.5″ colour	3″ colour
Internal memory	none	4 GB	32 GB	240 GB
Removable storage	SD card	none	SD card	SD card
Battery life	2.5 hours	2 hours	5 hours	3 hours
Extra features	waterproof, shockproof	none	none	GPS tagging
Wi-Fi	none	none	yes	none

Jill wants to buy a camcorder.

F (a) Which of these camcorders records at the highest resolution? **(1 mark)**

☐ Camcorder A

☐ Camcorder B

☐ Camcorder C

☒ Camcorder D

F (b) (i) Jill wants to record herself rock climbing.

Give **one** reason why Camcorder A is suitable. **(1 mark)**

it is Shockproof

> Think about features that would be particularly useful when filming outdoors or in dangerous locations.

E (ii) Jill needs extra removable storage for the camcorder.

State what she should buy. **(1 mark)**

SD/flash storage

F (c) Which of these camcorders would produce the best recordings of distant objects. **(1 mark)**

> **Guided**

~~☐ Camcorder A~~

☐ Camcorder B

☒ Camcorder C

☐ Camcorder D

> If you are not sure how to answer a question, then start by eliminating the answers you know are not right. So, for example, camcorder A has no zoom so it would not give good recordings of distant objects.

E (d) Most of the camcorders have an LCD screen.

State **one** use for the screen. **(1 mark)**

preview video + pictures

ICT DEPT MR GRANT

14 NOV 2013

Cameras and camcorders 2

Jill is enjoying a rock climbing and hiking holiday. She has taken a digital camera with her.

(F) **(a)** Jill's camera records the location where images are taken.

Which feature of the camera allows this data to be captured? **(1 mark)**

☐ **A** Wi-Fi

☐ **B** USB

☐ **C** 3G

☒ **D** GPS ✓

(G) **(b)** Jill wants to upload her images wirelessly. Which connectivity type would allow this?

(1 mark)

> **Guided**

☒ **A** Wi-Fi ✓

☐ **B** USB

☐ **C** Bluetooth

☐ **D** GPS

> If you are not sure, then start by crossing out the answers you know are wrong. For example, USB is not wireless so you can eliminate it.

(E-D) **(c)** Jill has uploaded some pictures to an online album for her friends to see.

Describe how Jill's friends might be able to use the location information attached to the images. **(2 marks)**

EXAM ALERT

Geotagging, this is providing the latitude + longitude to a picture. Metadata

> Students have struggled with exam questions similar to this – **be prepared!** ResultsPlus

(F-E) **(d)** Explain how Jill can control who can view her online albums. **(2 marks)**

By adding restrictions i.e, only friends, friends & family or everybody

ICT DEPT MR GRANT
2 2 NOV 2013

Media players 1

The table below shows the specifications of four personal media players.

	Media player A	Media player B	Media player C	Media player D
Interface	jog wheel	remote	multifunction button	touch screen
Connectivity	USB 1.0	USB 2.0	Bluetooth	Wi-Fi
Storage	500 MB	64 GB	160 GB	320 GB
Screen resolution	320 × 240	400 × 240	1280 × 720	640 × 480

Laura wants to buy a new media player.

(F)

(a) Which one of these can store the most data? **(1 mark)**

☐ Personal media player A

☐ Personal media player B

☐ Personal media player C

☒ Personal media player D

(F-E)

(b) Many personal media players offer security features.

Give **two** of these. **(2 marks)**

Guided

EXAM ALERT

1   They allow you to set a password which you have to enter correctly to unlock the device.

2   *facial recognition*

> This question is asking how you can protect the data on a personal media player. Make sure you give two **different** security features.

> This was a real exam question that a lot of students struggled with – **be prepared!** ResultsPlus

(G-F)

(c) List **two** peripheral devices that Laura could use with her personal media player. **(2 marks)**

1   *headphones*

2   *speaker/dock*

(F-E)

(d) Laura likes to download and watch movies and videos on her personal media player.

List **two** formats used for video and movie files. **(2 marks)**

1   *MP4*

2   *AVI*

(F)

(e) Laura wants to connect her personal media player to her television.

Which connection type would allow this? **(1 mark)**

ICT DEPT MR GRANT

2 2 NOV 2013

☐ **A** Serial

☐ **B** Infrared

☐ **C** PS/2

☒ **D** HDMI

Media players 2

Laura downloads music from Internet sites to her personal media player.

D-C
Guided

(a) (i) Explain why the MP3 format is suitable for downloading.   **(2 marks)**

The MP3 format uses less data to store the audio information which means that ....

more songs can be stored on the device

E

(ii) State **one** disadvantage to the listener of using the MP3 format.   **(1 mark)**

Sound quality

F

(iii) One of Laura's friends asks her to make a copy of the music files she has bought. State why she must not do this.   **(1 mark)**

copyright laws/DRM

(b) Laura likes to stream movies as well as to download them.

E-D

(i) Give **two** advantages to Laura of streaming movies rather than downloading them.   **(2 marks)**

1 *saves space on computer hard drive*

2 *Can be streamed directly to TV*

D-C

(ii) Give **two** disadvantages to Laura of streaming movies rather than downloading them.   **(2 marks)**

1 *Requires stable WiFi*

2 *Quality of the video can change*

ICT DEPT MR GRANT
2 2 NOV 2013

Games consoles 1

Emma enjoys playing computer games.

(a) Emma buys a new HD games console.

G

(i) State **one** other piece of equipment she will need to play games in HD. **(1 mark)**

.....HD TV.../.................................

....

> Think about the fact that a games console cannot actually display HD.

E-D

(ii) Emma thinks that games consoles are better than PCs for gaming.

State **two** advantages of using consoles, rather than PCs, for gaming. **(2 marks)**

> **Guided**

1 Consoles do not require much set up compared with PCs.

2 ...Not as expensive................................/.................

....

G-E

(iii) Give **three** peripherals that can be connected to a console. **(3 marks)**

1 ...headset../.....................

> Think about the peripherals that might enhance her gaming experience or allow her to use her games console for other things.

2 ...Controller................................/......................

3 ...USB...

F-E

(b) Modern games consoles are multifunctional devices.

Apart from gaming, give **two other** uses for games consoles. **(2 marks)**

1 ...Watching movies................................/...............

2 ...streaming...

(c) Many gaming companies allow users to download games straight to their consoles.

E

(i) Give **one** advantage to the company of allowing this. **(1 mark)**

dont have to go to a shop to buy it....../...............

....

D-B

(ii) Explain **one** environmental benefit of downloading games rather than buying them on disk. **(2 marks)**

less plastic waste, aswell as less
CD's being used/wasted

....

.................................ICT DEPT MR GRANT.................................

.................................2 2 NOV 2013........................../.............

─────────

Games consoles 2

D-C

(a) Emma plays games excessively and gets eye strain.

Give **two** possible ways to avoid eye strain. **(2 marks)**

> **Guided**

1   Make sure the screen is ..... low   brightness ..... ✓

2   Take frequent .. breaks

D-B

(b) Emma's parents worry that she may spend too much time game playing.

Explain the effects of excessive game playing. **(3 marks)**

Obesity, RSI, distance
between friends and
family.

> Many people make claims without having any evidence. This question is asking you to explain, with examples, how excessive gaming can affect people.

C-A*

(c) Give **three** ways in which playing violent and antisocial games might affect people's relationships with others. **(3 marks)**

1   May create distance between
friends and family

2   May cause you to easily get
aggressive

3   Might affect sentimental emotions

ICT DEPT MR GRANT ✓

2 2 NOV 2013

Home entertainment systems

Mr and Mrs Clark have signed up with a company that provides digital media content through a cable connection.

(a) The company provided them with a set top box.

F

    (i) State the function of the set top box. **(1 mark)**

recieves ~~satelite~~ satelite signal and displays video

E

    (ii) The set top box also contains a digital video recorder that allows them to record programmes to play back at a later date.

    State **one other** function they will be able to use the set top box for. **(1 mark)**

radio

D

    (iii) Apart from digital television channels, state one other service that the company can provide through the cable network. **(1 mark)**

radio

(b) The Clarks have bought the following home entertainment equipment:

HD digital television
Connectivity: HDMI and Wi-Fi

Blu-ray player
Connectivity: HDMI

Speakers
Connectivity: Wi-Fi

E-C

Describe how the Clarks could connect the devices to allow them to view a film and use the external speakers. **(3 marks)**

The TV can be connected to the blu-ray player using ~~HD~~ HDMI and the TV can be connected to the speakers through wifi

Satellite navigation 1

Shameela is driving to an area of London she has never visited before.

E

(a) (i) She has a sat nav device in her car. Sat nav devices use GPS.

State the function of GPS. **(1 mark)**

to get direction from one location to another

EXAM ALERT

This was a real exam question that a lot of students struggled with – **be prepared!** **ResultsPlus**

D

(ii) Shameela has her destination bookmarked in her sat nav.

State why bookmarking the location helps her. **(1 mark)**

> **Guided**

It saves Shameela time because *she can go to bookmarks and select the destination*

E-B

(iii) Describe **two** health and safety risks of using a sat nav while driving. **(4 marks)**

1 *It can distract her from her driving - could cause an accident*

2 *If the driver takes their eyes off their road something could happen*

E-D

(b) In addition to providing directions to a destination, give **two other** ways in which sat navs can aid drivers. **(2 marks)**

1 *give traffic reports*

2 *plot speeds*

Satellite navigation 2

E

(a) State **one** way in which sat navs can provide specialist help for disabled drivers. **(1 mark)**

It can display shops
+ facilities

> The question is asking how sat navs can provide 'specialist' help rather than general functions. So make sure you do not just give one of the general functions of sat navs, such as 'they help with route planning', because you will not get a mark.

F-E

(b) Smartphones are now multifunctional devices and most have GPS which can be used with sat nav apps.

Give **two** advantages of using a smartphone rather than a dedicated sat nav. **(2 marks)**

1 smartphone is always with you

2 only one job does the job, saves time

C-B

(c) Drivers do not need a dedicated hands-free kit if they have a Bluetooth-enabled sat nav. Explain why. **(2 marks)**

It can act as a hands free kit if the phone has bluetooth it can act as a loud speaker

Impact on organisations

 C-A*

*Discuss how business organisations have had to adapt their working practices in response to the increased use of personal digital devices. **(6 marks)**

This question has an asterisk which means that the quality of your written communication will be assessed. You need to think about your spelling, punctuation and grammar as well as clarity of expression. You should make a list of all the points you want to make and then plan out your answer before you start writing. Think about the effects of the increased use of personal digital devices on areas such as:
- employees using their personal digital devices for work
- remote working and collaboration
- cloud data storage
- security issues
- communicating with customers
- use of Internet and social networking.

Mobile phones allow workers to communicate with each other and customers at any time. Allows workers to collaborate with each other as it is easy to communicate. Also with wifi the use of the cloud is stronger as it can help with sharing files and documents between each of the employees.
The use of internet + social net networking.

Home networks

Mr and Mrs Green have decided to set up a home network for themselves and their two teenage children, Josh and Ben.

F-E

(a) State **two** benefits to the family of setting up a home network.   **(2 marks)**

Guided

1   Backing up data to another computer.

2   ....

....

> This question is asking for the benefits of installing a home network not the advantages of one type over another.

F

(b) To set up the network they have bought this item of hardware.

State the name of this item of hardware.   **(1 mark)**

....

(c) Mr and Mrs Green have decided that the family will use wireless connections.

F-E

(i) State **two** advantages of a wireless network over a wired one.   **(2 marks)**

1   ....

....

2   ....

....

D-C

(ii) Mr Green tries to access his Wi-Fi and notices that he has no signal.

Explain **one** cause of signal loss on Wi-Fi.   **(2 marks)**

....

....

....

....

> Make sure you give an explanation: make a point, then explain it.

C-B

(d) Josh and Ben decide to stream a HD film and connect the PC via Ethernet.

Explain why they connect the Ethernet cable to view this film.   **(2 marks)**

....

....

....

....

Network security

The Green family are now using their home network for work and entertainment.

C-B (a) Mr Green checks the wireless network and notices that a device that is not in the house is connected.

Explain how this other device could have connected to their wireless network. **(2 marks)**

⟩ **Guided** ⟩   *The network is unsecured which means that* ....

....

....

C (b) (i) State what Mr Green could do to prevent people discovering the name of his
network.   **(1 mark)**

....

.... | This question is asking you to apply what you know about how Wi-Fi routers advertise their presence.

....

C-B (ii) Explain how Mr Green could use MAC address filtering to prevent computers, other than those belonging to the family, from being able to connect to the network.

(2 marks)

....

....

....

....

(c) Mr Green turns on WPA.

G (i) Explain what WPA is a form of.   **(1 mark)**

....

C-B (ii) Explain how WPA will increase the security of the network.   **(2 marks)**

....

.... | In your answer you should explain what WPA does and how this will improve network security.

....

....

....

Combining technologies

Michael and Ryan are travelling abroad.

Ryan has taken his smartphone and Michael has taken his tablet computer as shown in Figure 1.

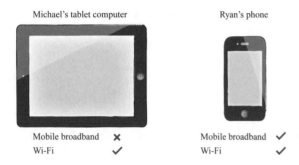

Michael's tablet computer   Ryan's phone

Mobile broadband ✗   Mobile broadband ✓
Wi-Fi ✓   Wi-Fi ✓

Figure 1

They are in an area where there is no Wi-Fi Internet access.

D-C

(a) Describe how Ryan could share his phone's mobile broadband connection with Michael's tablet without using cables. **(2 marks)**

Guided

Ryan could set up his phone as ....

....

....

> You need to describe how Ryan's phone can allow Michael's tablet to connect to it and share its 3G network.

....

....

F

(b) State how Ryan could prevent other devices from sharing his connection. **(1 mark)**

....

....

C-B

(c) Explain why sharing the connection might affect the bandwidth available to Ryan. **(2 marks)**

....

....

....

....

Bandwidth and latency

Laura carried out a ping test to check her new broadband connection. It showed that the latency of her connection is very low.

C-A

(a) Laura enjoys playing online games.

Explain how this low latency will affect her online gaming experience.   **(2 marks)**

....

....

....

....

....

....

> There are two marks for this question. You need to say whether the low latency will improve her gaming experience or not, and then give a reason for your answer.

F

(b) Laura's Internet Service Provider (ISP) claims that her broadband has a bandwidth of 30 Mb.

What does this figure mean?   **(1 mark)**

☐ **A** 30 megabytes per second

☐ **B** 30 megabytes per minute

☐ **C** 30 megabits per second

☐ **D** 30 megabits per minute

A-A*

(c) When Laura checks her bandwidth online she gets this result:

10.21 Mbps

Explain why her bandwidth is lower than the 30 Mbps her ISP advertises.   **(2 marks)**

....

....

....

....

C-B

EXAM ALERT

(d) Laura is downloading lots of files at the same time.

Explain why this could cause a slow download speed.   **(2 marks)**

....

....

....

> Students have struggled with exam questions similar to this – **be prepared!**   ResultsPlus

Wi-Fi and mobile broadband

Stephen is going on holiday and is taking his netbook computer as well as his mobile phone, so that he can keep in touch with his friends and watch videos while he is travelling.

(a) In the airport, Stephen's computer connects to an open Wi-Fi network.

F

    (i) Areas where you can connect to networks like this are called: **(1 mark)**

        ☐ **A** Mobile spots

        ☐ **B** Hotspots

        ☐ **C** Access spots

        ☐ **D** Internet spots

C-B

Guided

    (ii) Explain why open networks may pose a security risk.   **(2 marks)**

Hackers can set up ....

....

....

There are 2 marks for this question so you should include more than one simple statement in your answer.

....

(b) At the airport Stephen buys a dongle to allow him to connect to the Internet when Wi-Fi is not available.

G

    (i) The technology that allows his computer to use this network is called: **(1 mark)**

        ☐ **A** Open broadband

        ☐ **B** Fast broadband

        ☐ **C** Mobile broadband

        ☐ **D** Access broadband

D-C

    (ii) Give **two** benefits and **two** drawbacks of using 3G rather than Wi-Fi.   **(4 marks)**

        Benefits

EXAM ALERT

        1 ....

          ....

Make sure you don't confuse the different types of broadband available on your mobile phone.

        2 ....

          ....

Students have struggled with exam questions similar to this – **be prepared!** ResultsPlus

        Drawbacks

        1 ....

          ....

        2 ....

          ....

Peer-to-peer networks

John is transferring a music file from his mobile phone to his laptop using Bluetooth (see Figure 1).

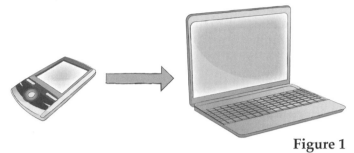

Figure 1

E (a) (i) Give **one** advantage of using Bluetooth over using Wi-Fi. **(1 mark)**

....

....

F-E (ii) Give **two other** ways John could transfer the file from his mobile phone to his laptop. **(2 marks)**

Guided

1 USB cable.

2 ....

.... | You are being asked to give two ways other than Bluetooth and Wi-Fi of transferring files between devices.

....

E-D (b) Erica works in a large office in which the computers are networked using Wi-Fi.

Explain why Wi-Fi is used and not Bluetooth. **(2 marks)**

....

....

....

....

You should explain why Bluetooth is not suitable in a large office where large amounts of data are being transferred.

Communication protocols 1

Katerina has a laptop and likes to communicate with her friends all over the world.

(F)

(a) She often makes voice calls to her friends over the Internet.

Which protocol are the computers using to make these calls? **(1 mark)**

- ☐ **A** HTTP
- ☐ **B** VoIP
- ☐ **C** SMTP
- ☐ **D** HTTPS

(G-F)

(b) List **two** peripherals that their computers might need to make these calls. **(2 marks)**

1 ....

2 ....

(A)

(c) Name the communication protocol most commonly used for sending emails. **(1 mark)**

....

(d) The IMAP protocol allows users to read emails on the mail server. Katerina's mail program uses the IMAP protocol.

(C-B)

(i) Give **one** benefit and **one** drawback to Katerina of using the IMAP protocol.

(2 marks)

Benefit

⟩ Guided ⟩

IMAP allows Katerina to access her inbox ....

....

Drawback

....

....

(B-A*)

(ii) Explain how the POP protocol handles emails differently from the IMAP protocol.

(2 marks)

....

....

....

....

....

....

> The question tells you that the IMAP protocol allows users to read emails on the mail server. Think about how the POP protocol is different. If it does not store emails on the mail server, where does it send them?

Communication protocols 2

Oliver likes to surf the web to find websites selling games online.

(a) Which protocol do websites use?   **(1 mark)**

....

(b) When Oliver has to enter his credit card details to make a purchase, the URL changes to green to indicate that the site is secure.

(i) State **one other** way that Oliver can check that the website is secure.   **(1 mark)**

....

(ii) Oliver can view the website's security certificate like the one shown in Figure 1.

Certificate	? ✕

General | Details | Certification Path

Certificate Information

This certificate is intended for the following purpose(s):
•Ensures the identity of a remote computer
*Refer to the certification authority's statement for details.

Issued to: www.pearsonschoolsandfecolleges.co.uk   **Issued by:** VeriSign Class 3 Secure Server CA - G3
Valid from: 24/03/2011 **to** 29/04/2013

Install Certificate...   Issuer Statement...

OK

Figure 1

Explain why security certificates are issued.   **(2 marks)**

> **Guided**

Digital certificates are issued by an authentication company to ....

....

....

....

(c) When you are connected to a secure website the data that is sent is encrypted.

Explain what is meant by 'encryption'.   **(2 marks)**

EXAM ALERT

....

....

....

....

....

....

There are 2 marks for this question which means that you need to give more than one statement. One way to approach this question would be to explain what one computer does to the data sent, and what the other computer does to understand the data.

Students have struggled with exam questions similar to this – **be prepared!**

ResultsPlus

Security risks in a network

Sam thinks he has a virus on his PC.

D

(a) (i) Sam installed antivirus software when he bought his computer last year.

Suggest a reason why it may not have prevented this virus infection. **(1 mark)**

....

....

B-A

(ii) Sam installs a firewall.

Explain why he does this. **(2 marks)**

....

....

....

....

E-D

(iii) Give **two** other precautions that Sam should take to prevent a virus infection when he is using the Internet. **(2 marks)**

〉Guided〉

1   He should try to avoid file-sharing websites.

2 ....

   ....

> Your answers must be related to using the Internet, and not to any other activity.

F-E

(b) When Sam is setting up online login accounts he is asked to create a password.

Give **two** features of a strong password. **(2 marks)**

1 ....

   ....

   ....

2 ....

   ....

> Make sure you give two different answers. For example, 'Don't just use letters' and 'Use a mix of letters and other characters' is actually the same point.

Physical security risks

DataProgramming is a large software company. They employ 60 programmers to develop software for other companies.

Discuss the security measures that *DataProgramming* should take at their offices.   **(6 marks)**

> This question has an asterisk which means that the quality of your written communication will be assessed. You need to think about your spelling, punctuation and grammar as well as clarity of expression. You should therefore plan out your answer before you start writing by making a list of all the points you want to make and putting those points in a logical order so that you present them in a clear way. Think about the following points:
> - physical security measures
> - ways of restricting access to systems
> - surveillance and monitoring.

....

....

....

....

....

....

....

....

....

....

....

....

....

....

....

....

....

....

The Internet

Many families set up home networks so that all family members can share a broadband Internet connection.

F

Guided

(a) Which protocol do web browsers use to view web pages? **(1 mark)**

☐ **A** TCP/IP

~~☐ **B** POP3~~

☐ **C** HTTP

☐ **D** HTML

> If you are not sure what the answer is, then start by crossing off the options you know are wrong. So, in this case, POP3 cannot be the right answer because it is a communication protocol used when receiving emails.

E

(b) State the device their computers must contain for them to be able to access the Internet through a home network. **(1 mark)**

....

(c) The table below shows the services offered by two Internet Service Providers.

	MyWeb	DWInternet
Bandwidth	8 Mbps	50 Mbps
Email addresses	2	10
Security	firewall	firewall
Parental controls	no	yes
Download limit	10GB	unlimited
Monthly charge	£5	£15

E-C

(i) Mr and Mrs Smith have three children. They all use the Internet for email, downloading and streaming movies and playing online games. They have chosen DWInternet.

Explain why this is the best choice for the family. **(3 marks)**

....

....

....

....

C-A

(ii) Both ISPs provide a firewall.

Explain how a firewall can improve online security. **(3 marks)**

....

....

....

....

Internet use 1

Ann is spending a year travelling around Europe and wants to tell her friends about her adventures and show them photos of the places she is visiting. She has taken her smartphone and a netbook computer with her.

F

(a) In some areas she does not have access to Wi-Fi. Give a different connectivity type she might use to access data using her smartphone. **(1 mark)**

....

D-C

(b) Ann sets up a blog to use while she is travelling. Describe what is meant by a blog. **(2 marks)**

Guided

A blog is a shared ....

....

People use blogs to ....

Other people can ....

E-D

(c) Ann has a choice of sending photos from her smartphone using MMS or by uploading them to her social networking site. Give **two** advantages of uploading to a social networking site over sending by MMS. **(2 marks)**

1 ....

....

2 ....

....

> Make sure you think about the context given in the question. Do not just give generic answers like 'quicker' **without explaining them** because you could miss out on valuable marks.

F-E

(d) Ann uploads her photos to her social networking site.

Give **two** ways in which she can control who can see the pictures. **(2 marks)**

1 ....

....

2 ....

....

F

(e) (i) Ann's netbook has a built-in webcam, microphone and speakers and she has used it to make voice and video calls to her friends. Give the protocol used to make free voice calls over the Internet. **(1 mark)**

....

C-B

(ii) During these calls to her friends, sometimes the person's voice 'breaks up' and sounds slurred. Explain why this may occur. **(2 marks)**

....

....

....

....

Internet use 2

The widespread use of the Internet has had an impact on the ways that organisations operate.

(a) Companies can use video conferencing hardware and software for business meetings.

E-D

   (i) List **two** benefits to a company of using video conferencing. **(2 marks)**

1 ....

....

2 ....

....

C-B

   (ii) List **two** disadvantages of using video conferencing rather than having face-to-face meetings. **(2 marks)**

> **Guided**

1 If the computers crash or the equipment fails, the meeting might have to be rescheduled.

2 ....

....

D-A*

(b) Describe how the use of the Internet has affected the ways in which students learn.

(3 marks)

....

....

....

....

....

....

Security measures

Sereena is opening an online account that she wants to be secure.

(G)

(a) (i) The account requires a password and Sereena is shown that hers is not very secure.

Which **one** of these passwords is the most secure? **(1 mark)**

☐ **A** seahorse

☐ **B** C-hor4se

☐ **C** Chor4se

☐ **D** C-horse

> You need to apply what you know about the features of strong passwords.

(F)

(ii) Sereena is asked to enter her new password twice.

Give **one** reason for this. **(1 mark)**

> **Guided**

This is to check that Sereena ....

....

(E-D)

EXAM ALERT

(iii) Sereena is asked if she wants the system to remember her password.

Explain why this might not be a good thing to do. **(2 marks)**

....

....

....

....

> Be sure to explain the point you make.

> This was a real exam question that a lot of students struggled with – **be prepared!** ResultsPlus

(E-D)

(b) Sereena has selected a secret question and provided an answer to it.

Explain why she has been asked to do this. **(2 marks)**

....

....

....

(F)

(c) To finish setting up the account Sereena is asked to enter the letters she sees:

WpZ729XF 🔊 ⇕

☐

Enter the 8 characters you see

This is used to:

☐ **A** test the computer's screen resolution **(1 mark)**

☐ **B** prevent automated sign-up scripts

☐ **C** stop people from guessing Sereena's password

☐ **D** test how good Sereena's eye sight is

Personal spaces

James has his own 'personal spaces' on his school's Virtual Learning Environment (VLE) and a social networking site.

E-C

(a) Describe how a VLE can be used by students, teachers and parents to enhance traditional learning. **(3 marks)**

....

....

....

....

....

....

G-F

Guided

(b) James was able to personalise his area on the school's VLE by adding pictures.

List **two other** things that James can do to personalise his online spaces. **(2 marks)**

1   He could add text, such as ....

....

2   He could add ....

....

E-D

(c) James wants to protect his privacy online.

Describe **two** things James can do to protect his privacy when online. **(2 marks)**

1   ....

....

2   ....

....

D-C

(d) Describe what James should do if he discovers that a user has posted an offensive message about him on an online forum. **(2 marks)**

....

....

....

....

Information misuse

Jane likes to buy clothes online and has set up accounts with suppliers. She is worried that her personal details might not be kept securely.

G-F

(a) List **two** items of personal information that Jane will have to submit when she is setting up an online account. **(2 marks)**

1 ....

2 ....

E-D

(b) Jane has just bought a pair of jeans. The booking screen displays Jane's card number as shown in Figure 1:

Card number   **** **** **** ****

Figure 1

Explain why the card number is displayed like this. **(2 marks)**

....

....

....

....

F

(c) Criminals often remotely install software on PCs.

State the name of this kind of software. **(1 mark)**

....

B-A

Guided

(d) Explain why most malware / Trojans need human involvement to install them. **(3 marks)**

Most computer security software is very strong so hackers and criminals rely on ....

....

....

....

....

Preventing misuse

G

(a) When we visit websites they often download small text files to our computers to track what we do on the site.

State the name of these text files. **(1 mark)**

....

D-C

(b) Reputable firms will have a privacy policy displayed on their website.

State **two** things that a privacy policy tells you. **(2 marks)**

Guided

1   What information the company is collecting about you.

EXAM ALERT

2   ....

> Students have struggled with exam questions similar to this – **be prepared!** ResultsPlus

D-C

(c) One method criminals use to find out our personal details is spyware.

Give **two** precautions users should take to prevent spyware being downloaded to their computers. **(2 marks)**

1   ....

....

2   ....

....

(d) Some criminals send bogus emails like the one shown below to trick computer users into telling them their personal and financial details.

F

(i) What do we call this type of email? **(1 mark)**

Dear Customer,
Due to recent system upgrades, we urgently need you to confirm your acount details by clicking on the link below:
http://www.azbookshop.co.uk/account/login
We may also request in a seperate email message scanned copies of one or more forms of photo ID.
If you don't follow the link and confirm your details within the next 36 hours, we reserve the right to terminate your account. This will leave you unable to make online puchases with us.
Yours,
AZbooks team

☐   **A** virus

☐   **B** Trojan

☐   **C** phishing

☐   **D** spyware

E-D

(ii) State **two** clues that might suggest that it is a bogus email. **(2 marks)**

1   ....

2   ....

Legislation

Anya is concerned that personal details she has given about herself to online sites might not be secure.

D-C

(a) (i) List **two** reasons why data stored online might not be as secure as data stored in paper-based systems in offices. **(2 marks)**

Guided

1 Digital files can be copied more easily than paper files.

2 ....

....

> Think about what would be involved in physically breaking into an office and stealing paper files.

F

(ii) What is the name of the act that organisations have to comply with if they store personal details on the computer? **(1 mark)**

....

E-B

(iii) State **two** ways in which organisations can prevent unauthorised access to the data they store. **(2 marks)**

1 ....

....

2 ....

....

D-C

(iv) List **two** demands that Anya can make of the organisations storing her data. **(2 marks)**

1 ....

....

2 ....

....

C-A

(b) The Computer Misuse Act was introduced in 1990.

Explain why the Computer Misuse Act was introduced. **(3 marks)**

EXAM ALERT

....

....

....

....

....

....

> Knowledge of legislation is often poor. Make sure you understand what companies can and can't do with the data collected and stored. Students often confuse legislation with security.

> Students have struggled with exam questions similar to this – **be prepared!** ResultsPlus

Copyright

D-B   **(a)** There are many file sharing websites where music is distributed illegally.

Explain the impact illegal file sharing has on the music industry.   **(3 marks)**

....

....

....

....

....

....

G   **(b)** If you download music from an illegal site which act are you breaking?   **(1 mark)**

☐   **A**   The Data Protection Act

☐   **B**   The Computer Misuse Act

☐   **C**   The Copyright, Designs and Patents Act

☐   **D**   The Computer Downloading Act

E-D   **(c)** Although illegal sites may harm the music industry, many musicians benefit from selling their music online through legal sites.

List **two** benefits to musicians of selling their music online.   **(2 marks)**

> **Guided**

1   Musicians do not need a record company to be able to produce and sell music.

2   ....

....

(d) Jo searches the Internet for images to illustrate her school project. She finds some images that allow use for non-commercial purposes.

B-A

EXAM ALERT

   (i) Explain Jo's legal responsibilities for the use of these images.   **(2 marks)**

....

....

....

....

> Think carefully about what this question is asking. Jo can use the images for her school project but what must she do if she uses them?

> Students have struggled with exam questions similar to this – **be prepared!**   ResultsPlus

C-B   **(ii)** Jo finds some images that she wants to use in a book she intends to sell. Explain what Jo would have to do if she were to use these images.   **(2 marks)**

....

....

....

....

Online shopping 1

Salim has always bought CDs in a shop but now he is thinking of buying them online instead.

E

(a) (i) Which **one** of these statements about online shopping is true? **(1 mark)**

☐ **A** Shopping online always involves purchasing a physical object.

☐ **B** Online shops always sell goods that are available on the high street.

☐ **C** Goods bought online may not be returned.

☐ **D** Some services and goods are now only available for purchase online.

D-C

Guided

(ii) Give **two** features of an online shop that will help Salim buy the CDs. **(2 marks)**

1 He will be able to read other customers' reviews.

2 ....

> Remember to think of the situation which is asked – give comments that are relevant to buying CDs.

D-C

(b) Salim would like to buy a cheap railway ticket.

Give **two** features of an online booking system that will help him buy his ticket.

(2 marks)

1 ....

....

2 ....

....

C-B

(c) Explain how the Internet has impacted on how individuals buy and sell online. **(3 marks)**

....

....

....

....

....

Online shopping 2

D-C

EXAM ALERT

(a) Catherine buys a dress online.

(i) Give **two** advantages to Catherine of buying clothes online.   **(2 marks)**

1 ....

....

2 ....

....

> Students have struggled with exam questions similar to this – **be prepared!** ResultsPlus

C

(ii) Give **two** disadvantages to Catherine of buying clothes online.   **(2 marks)**

1 ....

....

2 ....

....

> The question is about buying clothes. Therefore the answers should be about clothes and will be different to buying other products such as groceries.

B

Guided

(b) Catherine's dress arrives safely and in perfect condition. She does not like the colour. Explain Catherine's consumer rights.   **(2 marks)**

Catherine has the right to return the dress up to .... after receiving

it. She is entitled to ....

....

(c) David sells toys in his high street shop and online.

B

(i) Give **two** benefits to David of closing the high street shop and only selling online.

(2 marks)

1 ....

....

2 ....

....

> Remember that David already sells online and so you must state the benefits of not having a high street shop rather than the benefits of selling online.

E

(ii) State **one** group of people who might find it more accessible to shop online rather than on the high street.   **(1 mark)**

....

....

....

Online auctions

(a) Paul has finished his exams. He wants to sell his revision notes.

D-A
Guided

(i) Describe how he could use an online auction site to do this. **(3 marks)**

First of all, Paul would need to create an online account

with the auction website. Then, he ....

....

> You need to think about the steps involved in selling an item on an online auction site.

....

....

....

....

E

(ii) Give **one** advantage to Paul of using an online auction website to sell his notes rather than selling them at a local shop or library. **(1 mark)**

....

....

E-D

(b) Paul also wants to buy some rare football cards for his collection.

Explain **one** advantage to Paul of buying them from an online auction rather than a high street store. **(2 marks)**

....

....

....

....

Online education, news and banking

C–A*

EXAM ALERT

*Discuss the impact of the Internet on the use of news and information services.   **(6 marks)**

....
....
....
....
....
....
....
....
....
....
....
....
....

This question has an asterisk which means that the quality of your written communication will be assessed. You need to think about your spelling, punctuation and grammar as well as clarity of expression. You should make a list of all the points you want to make and then plan out your answer before you start writing. You must give a balanced argument, so don't forget to include negative impacts as well as positive ones. You might like to consider the following points:

- who can publish news and whether or not this is a good thing
- how available the material is
- the speed at which news and information is available
- the cost
- interactivity
- potential dangers.

....
....
....
....
....
....
....
....
....

Online gaming and entertainment

Kate watches TV online using on-demand streaming entertainment services.

E-D

(a) Give **two** features of on-demand entertainment services. **(2 marks)**

> **Guided**

1   Available on mobile devices.

2   ....

....

> Remember that on-demand streaming entertainment services allow us to choose when we watch TV programmes.

C-A

(b) Explain the difference between 'streaming' and 'downloading' a TV programme. **(4 marks)**

....

....

....

....

....

....

....

....

....

C-A

(c) Kate's Internet connection has low bandwidth.

Explain how this could affect her experience of streaming video. **(3 marks)**

....

....

....

....

....

....

How and why organisations operate online

Andrew has just set up a new company called *HandyPrint*.

HandyPrint sells printed products online.

D

(a) Give **one** disadvantage to *HandyPrint* of selling online. **(1 mark)**

> **Guided**

Andrew will need a secure ....

....

C

(b) Give **one** advantage to *HandyPrint* of selling online. **(1 mark)**

....

....

C-B

(c) Explain why selling online can be more profitable than owning a physical high street shop. **(3 marks)**

....

....

....

....

....

....

> Note that selling prices are often lower in online shops than on the high street, which will lower the profit.

C

(d) Give **one** reason why a high street shop might also want to open an online shop. **(1 mark)**

....

....

Had a go ☐ Nearly there ☐ Nailed it! ☐

Transactional data

Nikita is buying a pair of jeans from her favourite online clothes shop.

C-B

(a) List **two** pieces of transactional data that may be stored when she makes her purchase.

(2 marks)

> **Guided**

1 Date and time of purchase.

2 ....

....

> Transactional data contains information about your online purchases. Online organisations use it for targeted marketing and personalised adverts.

B-A

(b) Give **two** ways in which the transactional data may be useful **to Nikita**. **(2 marks)**

EXAM ALERT

1 ....

....

> Students have struggled with exam questions similar to this – **be prepared!** ResultsPlus

2 ....

....

C-A*

(c) Describe the impact that collecting transactional data has on companies. **(3 marks)**

....

....

....

....

Internet advertising 1

EasyFly is a new airline company. They use Internet advertising.

F-D

(a) Describe **one** benefit to *EasyFly* of advertising on the Internet rather than on television.

(2 marks)

....

....

....

....

D-A*

(b) *EasyFly* decides to place advertisements on search engines.

Explain how search engine advertisements can target people who might be interested in *EasyFly*.

(3 marks)

Guided

Search engine advertisements work by displaying adverts when users type relevant key

words into the search engine. Easyfly could carefully choose ....

....

....

....

....

A-A*

(c) *EasyFly* also advertises on social networks.

Social networks allow people to share content quickly and easily.

Explain **one other** reason why *EasyFly* would benefit from advertising on social networks.

(3 marks)

....

....

....

....

Internet advertising 2

A new music group called *MixUp* uses viral marketing to promote its latest album.

B

(a) State **one** feature of viral marketing. **(1 mark)**

....

....

....

> Think specifically about what makes viral marketing different to advertising in magazines.

C-B

(b) Describe **one** advantage to *MixUp* of using viral marketing rather than advertising in magazines. **(2 marks)**

....

....

....

....

> Remember: viral marketing, targeted marketing and personalisation techniques are all about trying to persuade people to buy things!

B-A

> Guided

(c) Describe how *MixUp* might use targeted marketing to promote their album. **(2 marks)**

MixUp could collect and combine online data from ....

....

to identify ....

> **Targeted** marketing is about concentrating the adverts on groups of customers who are most likely to buy a product.

They could then ....

....

....

....

....

Internet advertising 3

Martin is looking at an online music store.

C-A*

(a) Describe **two** personalisation techniques that could be used to target the content at Martin. **(4 marks)**

Guided

1   The website could compile 'favourites' for Martin based on his interests.

2   ....

....

D-C

(b) Give **two** advantages **to Martin** of receiving personalised advertising on the music website. **(2 marks)**

1   ....

....

2   ....

....

C

(c) Give **one** disadvantage **to Martin** of receiving personalised advertising on the music website. **(1 mark)**

....

....

D-C

(d) Give **two** ways in which Martin might avoid receiving personalised advertising in future. **(2 marks)**

1   ....

....

2   ....

....

Payment systems 1

Abdul is using a credit card to make an online payment on an auction website.

F

(a) He is asked to enter the CCV code.

Which **one** of these is the CCV code? **(1 mark)**

☐ A
☐ B
☐ C
☐ D

HLS Credit Card

A
2937 8162 9273 9723
06/07   06/10
B

C
D

C-B

(b) Explain **one** reason why Abdul needs to enter the CCV code. **(2 marks)**

> **Guided**

Entering the CCV means the person entering the code ....

....

....

....

E-D

(c) List **two** things Abdul should check on the web page before paying by credit card. **(2 marks)**

1 ....

....

2 ....

....

C-A

(d) The website Abdul is using says it is using Secure Sockets Layer (SSL).

Explain why Secure Sockets Layer is of benefit to Abdul. **(2 marks)**

....

....

....

....

> There are 2 marks available for this question. The first mark is available for saying what Secure Sockets Layer is and the second mark is for saying why it is of benefit. 'Explain' or 'Describe' questions often require you to show that you recall something **and then expand your point**, for example by giving reasons for its use.

Payment systems 2

Abdul would like to use his online banking account to make online payments.

C

(a) Give **two** ways the transaction will be kept secure. **(2 marks)**

> **Guided**

1   The bank will check that his account doesn't show any unusual activity.

> Think of the precautions the bank will take to protect Abdul's account.

2 ....

....

(b) Abdul has found out that he can use a third party processor to make his online payments.

D

   (i) Give **one** advantage **to Abdul** of using a third party payment processor. **(1 mark)**

....

....

B

   (ii) Give **one** advantage **to the retailer** of using a third party payment processor.

(1 mark)

....

> Third party payment processors act as a 'middle man' between the buyers and the sellers.

....

....

E-C

(c) Abdul has just purchased a smartphone with near field communication (NFC). He can pay for items in shops that have NFC readers.

Give **two** benefits to Abdul of paying using near field communication. **(2 marks)**

1 ....

....

2 ....

....

Consumer protection

C-A (a) Sarah buys a T-shirt from an online shop in the UK.

When it arrives she sees that the material is damaged. Explain Sarah's rights.   **(2 marks)**

> **Guided**

She has the same rights as in a high street shop so she can ....

....

....

....

B-A (b) Sarah buys some boots from a different website based in another country.

Explain why she may not have the right to return them.   **(2 marks)**

....

....

....

....

C (c) Sarah buys flowers online. When they arrive she does not like the colour.

State why she does not have the right to return them.   **(1 mark)**

....

....

D-C (d) Give **two** ways in which people are protected when they buy goods and services online.
   (2 marks)

EXAM ALERT

1 ....

....

2 ....

....

> Students have struggled with exam questions similar to this – **be prepared!**   ResultsPlus

Applications software

Jack wants to buy some software for his new online business.

(a) He could use either locally installed software or hosted software.

B

(i) State what is meant by hosted software. **(1 mark)**

> Guided

Hosted software runs on a ....

E–D

(ii) State **two** benefits to Jack of using hosted software. **(2 marks)**

> Guided

1 It can be accessed from ....

2 It doesn't take up much .... on your computer's ....

C–B

(iii) State **two** drawbacks to Jack of using hosted software. **(2 marks)**

1 ....

2 ....

E–C

(b) Jack reads a review of the software on the software company's own website.

He is worried the review may be biased.

Give **three other** sources of information he could use online. **(3 marks)**

1 ....

2 ....

3 ....

(c) Jack's friend recommends open source software.

D

(i) State what is meant by open source. **(1 mark)**

EXAM ALERT

....

....

....

> Students have struggled with exam questions similar to this – **be prepared!** ResultsPlus

> Be careful not to confuse **hosted software** with open source software.

F

(ii) State **one** benefit to Jack of using open source software. **(1 mark)**

....

....

D

(iii) State **one** drawback to Jack of using open source software. **(1 mark)**

....

....

Commercial response to SaaS

Jason is leaving home to start a new job and has just bought a new computer. He cannot decide whether to buy commercial software or to use software as a service.

B-A

Guided

(a) Give **two** features of software as a service.   **(2 marks)**

1   Contains applications such as ....

2   The applications are accessed ....

....

B-A

(b) Describe **one** way that commercial software producers could respond to the challenge of free software as a service.   **(2 marks)**

....

....

....

....

53

Storage: local or online?

Jason cannot decide whether to store his data locally or online.

F-D **(a)** His job requires him to work in several different offices during the week.

State **two** benefits to Jason of using online storage rather than local storage. **(2 marks)**

1 ....

....

2 ....

....

F-C **(b)** Give **two** drawbacks to Jason of online storage. **(2 marks)**

›Guided›

1 Jason has less control of his data as he does not know where it is stored.

2 ....

....

F **(c)** Jason decides to keep some video files on local storage in order to edit them when he has no Internet connection.

State why it is better to store these files on a DVD rather than a CD. **(1 mark)**

....

....

Search engines

Simon has been given a geography assignment to find out about the effects of earthquakes in Africa. He wants to use a search engine to find out the information he needs.

He searches for 'earthquakes' and gets the following results:

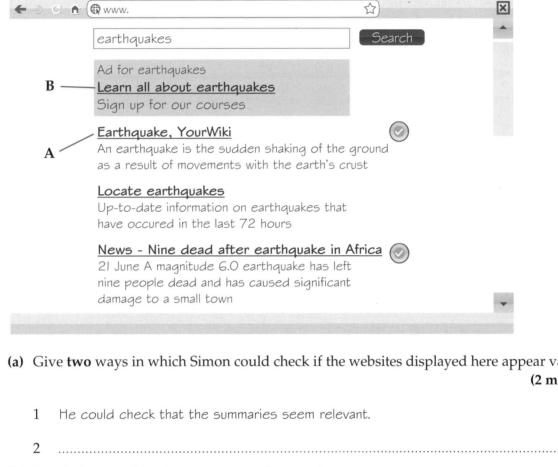

F-E

(a) Give **two** ways in which Simon could check if the websites displayed here appear valid.

(2 marks)

Guided

1   He could check that the summaries seem relevant.

2   ....

E

(b) Result A is a wiki, where users contribute to the content.

Give **one** reason why Simon should be concerned about the reliability of the information he finds. **(1 mark)**

....

....

E-D

(c) Explain why result B is at the top of the list in a shaded box. **(2 marks)**

....

....

....

D-C

(d) Some of the websites are not relevant to Africa.

Give **two** methods Simon could use to refine his search. **(2 marks)**

Guided

1   Add more key words to narrow down the search.

2   ....

....

Online communities – what are they?

Mel is a member of two online communities.

She uses a social networking website with friends and family and a Virtual Learning Environment for school.

C-B

Guided

EXAM ALERT

(a) Give **two** advantages to Mel of communicating with friends and family using social networking technology rather than SMS. **(2 marks)**

> Students have struggled with exam questions similar to this – **be prepared!** ResultsPlus

1   She only has to post one message to reach all her friends rather than sending lots of different ones.

2   ....

....

....

....

D-C

(b) Social networking websites and Virtual Learning Environments are types of online communities.

List **two other** types of online communities. **(2 marks)**

1   ....

....

2   ....

....

B-A*

(c) Social networking websites and Virtual Learning Environments have different features.

Explain why their features are different. **(3 marks)**

....

....

....

....

Online workspaces and VLEs

(a) Charlie is working on a report with a company in California using an online workspace.

C-B

Guided

  (i) State **two** features of an online workspace. **(2 marks)**

    1 Shared folders and files.

    2 ....

    ....

    ....

> Remember that an online workspace is for linking people who work together so that they can collaborate. Features are important 'areas' of the workspace.

EXAM ALERT

> Students have struggled with exam questions similar to this – **be prepared!** ResultsPlus

B

  (ii) The online workspace allows staff at both companies to work on the same documents in spite of the time difference.

    Give **one other** advantage of the online workspace to the staff.

    ....

    ....

(b) Oakfield School has just introduced a new Virtual Learning Environment (VLE).

D-C

  (i) List **two** features of a VLE that could be used by teachers. **(2 marks)**

    1 ....

    2 ....

D

  (ii) Parents at Oakfield School view event updates on the school's VLE.

    Give **one other** way that parents could use the school's VLE. **(1 mark)**

    ....

> Remember: Virtual Learning Environments allow students to work together to access lesson content, assessment tools and feedback, allowing them to work at their own pace.
> You also need to know how parents and teachers use VLEs.

Social networks

Joe is a photographer. His manager tells him to join a social network for photographers.

C
Guided

(a) List **two** features of social networks that Joe could use for work. **(2 marks)**

1 Sharing photos: Joe could share his photos with clients and other photographers.

2 ....

D-C

(b) Joe has heard that people have been bullied on their social networking pages.

List **two** other potential risks of communicating on social networks. **(2 marks)**

1 ....

....

....

2 ....

> Social networking is about linking people using personal information. You need to know the **advantages** and **disadvantages** of social networking.

....

....

B-A

(c) Give **two** advantages to Joe of using social networks, rather than email, to stay in touch with friends. **(2 marks)**

EXAM ALERT

1 ....

....

> Students have struggled with exam questions similar to this – **be prepared!** ResultsPlus

....

2 ....

....

C-A

(d) Explain why features on Joe's photography social network might be different from those he uses with friends and family. **(3 marks)**

....

....

....

....

....

....

User-generated reference sites

Anton is an interior designer. He is asked to use a wiki to share information with his colleagues.

C-B
⟩Guided⟩

(a) Describe **one** feature of a wiki that Anton could use. **(2 marks)**

The feature that allows all users to add and edit content in a simple web browser will

allow Anton to ....

....

....

D-B

(b) List **two** advantages to Anton of using a wiki rather than email for sharing information.

(2 marks)

1 ....

....

2 ....

....

> Remember: your answer must include an advantage of wikis over email, not a general use of wikis.

C-A

(c) A wiki is an example of a user-generated reference site.

Give **one other** example of a user-generated reference site and state its function. **(2 marks)**

Example ....

....

Function ....

....

Had a go ☐   Nearly there ☐   Nailed it! ☐

Social bookmarking sites

B

(a) State how social bookmarking websites are different from wikis. **(1 mark)**

> Guided

Users add ....

rather than .... ,

then ....

> Remember, social bookmarking websites allow people to store, share, tag and search for URLs.

(b) Sally is doing her Art project and is using a friend's 'pinboard' on a social bookmarking website.

C-B

(i) Explain **one** advantage to Sally of using a social bookmarking website rather than finding information with a search engine. **(2 marks)**

....

....

....

....

B

(ii) Give **one** possible problem of using information found on her friend's social bookmarking site. **(1 mark)**

....

....

Creation of knowledge

C-A* *Discuss the impact of the Internet on the way knowledge is created.   **(6 marks)**

....

....

....

....

....

....

....

....

....

....

> This question has an asterisk which means that the quality of your written communication will be assessed. You need to think about your spelling, punctuation and grammar as well as clarity of expression. You should make a list of all the points you want to make and then plan out your answer before you start writing. You must give a balanced argument, so don't forget to include negative impacts as well as positive ones. You might like to consider the following points:
> - who can create knowledge
> - how and with whom the knowledge is shared
> - the quality and accuracy of the knowledge.

....

....

....

....

....

....

....

....

....

....

....

....

....

....

Impact on working practices

Alexandria works for a university and has been told that she can telework from home for part of the week.

E-C

Guided

(a) Give **two** benefits to Alexandria of teleworking. **(2 marks)**

1   It will save her money.

2   ....

   ....

> The question tells you that teleworking will allow Alexandria to work from home. So don't give 'Can work from home' as one of your answers.

D-B

(b) Give **two** drawbacks to Alexandria of teleworking. **(2 marks)**

1   ....

   ....

2   ....

   ....

B-A

(c) Alexandria's university enables students to post and discuss course material online. Describe **two other** benefits the Internet has on learning. **(2 marks)**

1   ....

   ....

2   ....

   ....

E-C

(d) State **two** benefits of collaborative working. **(2 marks)**

1   ....

   ....

2   ....

   ....

E-C

(e) List **two** ways in which Alexandria could use the Internet to work collaboratively from home. **(2 marks)**

1   ....

   ....

2   ....

   ....

> Remember that ICT has both benefits and drawbacks on employment and working practices.

Socialising and responsible use

D-C

(a) Rageiv likes to socialise on the Internet.

List **two** ways in which Rageiv can be a 'responsible user'. **(2 marks)**

Guided

1   Honouring copyright laws by not making unauthorised copies of files.

2   ....

....

....

> Remember: being a responsible user is about demonstrating acceptable behaviour when using the Internet.

EXAM ALERT

> Students have struggled with exam questions similar to this – **be prepared!** ResultsPlus

C-A*

*(b) Discuss the benefits and drawbacks of using the Internet for socialising. **(6 marks)**

....

....

....

....

....

....

....

....

....

....

....

> This question has an asterisk which means that the quality of your written communication will be assessed. You need to think about your spelling, punctuation and grammar as well as clarity of expression.
> To answer questions like this well, you will need to give a balanced argument, showing both benefits and drawbacks. Make sure you plan your answer and think about how you will link your points together using joining phrases like: as well as, furthermore, besides, since, because, as a consequence, despite, whereas. You could write about your own experience of socialising online in your answer, but don't forget to think about other people's experiences as well.

....

....

....

....

....

....

....

A global scale

C-A* *'Globalisation refers to the increasing global relationships of culture, people, and economic activity.'

Discuss the impact of using ICT on a global scale. **(6 marks)**

EXAM ALERT

....

....

....

....

....

....

....

....

....

....

....

....

....

....

....

....

....

....

....

....

....

....

This question has an asterisk which means that the quality of your written communication will be assessed. You need to think about your spelling, punctuation and grammar as well as clarity of expression.

To answer questions like this well, you will need to give a balanced argument, showing both positive and negative impacts. Make sure you plan your answer and think about how you will link your points together.

You could think about the impacts of using ICT on a global scale in the following areas:
- communication and collaboration
- availability of goods and services
- business.

Students have struggled with exam questions similar to this – **be prepared!** ResultsPlus

Security issues

RedRose, a new company selling online flowers, is concerned that their main server computer has been hacked.

D

(a) State what is meant by hacking. **(1 mark)**

....

E-D

(b) List **two other** possible threats to the security of *RedRose*'s data. **(2 marks)**

> **Guided**

1   Physical threats, for example flooding and theft.

2   ....

(c) *RedRose* decides to back up their data.

E-C

(i) Explain why they do this. **(2 marks)**

....

....

E-C

(ii) Give **two other** ways *RedRose* can prevent security risks to their digital devices. **(2 marks)**

1   ....

2   ....

RedRose has a bank account with GlobalBank. *RedRose* receives the following email:

To: Sally@redroseflowers.co.uk
From: CustomerSupport@verify-globalbank.com
Dear Valued Customer
Due to security concerns, you are requested to submit additional details on your account.
Starting next week, we will be introducing new security measures that require this new information. Failure to update you're details to comply with these measures **within 72 hours** may result in you're account being frozen or suspended in order to protect your data.
Please be assured that GlobalBank works day and night to ensure your account is secure. Please have you're username and password to hand as you will need to confirm these so that we can verify that you are indeed the accountholder.
Please help us to help keep YOU'RE money safe.
Click here to update you're details. http://111.222.333.sam.banks.globalbank.htm
GlobalBank Customer Support

E-D

(d) List **two** things in this email which suggest it is not actually from GlobalBank. **(2 marks)**

1   ....

2   ....

D-B

(e) This email is an example of phishing.

Explain why phishing is a security risk to *RedRose*. **(2 marks)**

....

....

Privacy issues

C-A* *An online business collects details of its customers so that it can recommend relevant products. Discuss the privacy issues associated with shopping online.

(6 marks)

EXAM ALERT

....

....

....

....

....

....

....

....

....

....

This question has an asterisk which means that the quality of your written communication will be assessed. You need to think about your spelling, punctuation and grammar as well as clarity of expression.

You could think about areas such as:
- overt data collection
- covert data collection
- responsibilities businesses have to keep their customers' data safe.

Students have struggled with exam questions similar to this – **be prepared!** ResultsPlus

....

....

....

....

....

....

....

....

....

....

....

....

....

*

Monitoring movements and communications

C-A

(a) Soldiers have been warned not to upload geotagged images to social networks.

Explain why uploading geotagged images could pose a risk to soldiers.   **(2 marks)**

Guided

EXAM ALERT

Geotagging information gives an exact location. 'Friends'

in social networks are not ....

....

> Geotagging information gives an exact location. What makes this particularly risky for soldiers?

> Students have struggled with exam questions similar to this – **be prepared!**   ResultsPlus

C-A*

*(b) The benefits of using technology to track movement and communication outweigh the risks.

Make a reasoned argument to support this point of view.   **(6 marks)**

....

....

....

....

....

....

....

....

....

....

....

....

....

> This question has an asterisk which means that the quality of your written communication will be assessed. You need to think about your spelling, punctuation and grammar as well as clarity of expression.
>
> Note that this question requires you to **support a point of view** rather than present a balanced argument. When answering this type of question:
>
> 1 Give points that support the point of view, explaining each point with examples.
> 2 Show that you are aware of opposing points of view.
> 3 Reiterate that the arguments supporting the point of view are stronger than those against it.
> 4 Summarise why the point of view given is valid.
>
> Remember: it doesn't matter if you don't agree with the point of view presented. You still need to make a reasoned argument to support it.

....

....

....

Health and safety

E-D

Guided

(a) Pete is concerned about the effect that ICT may have on his family.

State **two** possible health issues resulting from the use of ICT. **(2 marks)**

1   Repetitive strain injuries can develop from doing the same thing/movement again and
    again.

2   ....

    ....

D-C

(b) Pete's family has just bought a games console so they can play together.

Give **two** ways in which ICT can help to improve the family's health. **(2 marks)**

1   ....

    ....

2   ....

    ....

D-C

(c) Explain the importance of using hands-free devices while driving. **(2 marks)**

....

....

....

....

The impact of networks

C-A* *Faster broadband speeds and more widespread mobile phone coverage mean we live in a connected world. Networks are now available anywhere and anytime.

Discuss how the widespread use of networks has impacted on both individuals and society.

(6 marks)

> This question has an asterisk which means that the quality of your written communication will be assessed. You need to think about your spelling, punctuation and grammar as well as clarity of expression. You need to give a balanced argument which considers both positive **and negative** impacts of networks on individuals and society. You might like to think about impacts on:
> - work
> - shopping
> - communication
> - creativity
> - those who can't access networks.

Legislation relating to the use of ICT

C

Guided

(a) Which **one** of the following offences would be prosecuted under the Computer Misuse Act? **(1 mark)**

☐ **A** Planting viruses

☐ **B** Downloading copyrighted material

~~☐ **C** Copying images~~

☐ **D** Copying software without a licence

> Eliminate the answers you know aren't right. Illegal copying is dealt with by a different act.

E–A

EXAM ALERT

(b) Give **one other** example of legislation relating to the use of ICT and explain how it protects our digital information. **(3 marks)**

....

....

....

....

....

....

....

....

> Remember to think about a variety of threats with examples and to discuss how the example of legislation covers different issues.

> Students have struggled with exam questions similar to this – **be prepared!** ResultsPlus

Unequal access to ICT

James cannot afford to have Internet access or a mobile phone.

C-A

Guided

(a) Describe **two** implications this has for James.   **(4 marks)**

1   James will have fewer IT skills so ....

....

....

2   James will have less access to online information

which means ....

....

> There are 2 marks for each point, so remember to make two different points and explain each one. For this question think about what James will miss out on without Internet access and a mobile phone and why that could be important to him.

C-A*

EXAM ALERT

*(b) Discuss the impact of the digital divide, both locally and globally.   **(6 marks)**

....

....

....

....

....

....

....

....

....

....

....

....

....

....

....

....

....

....

> Students have struggled with exam questions similar to this – **be prepared!**   ResultsPlus

> Remember that the **digital divide** is the gap between people who do not have access to digital technology and those who do.

> This question has an asterisk which means that the quality of your written communication will be assessed. You need to think about your spelling, punctuation and grammar as well as clarity of expression. You need to give a balanced argument which considers both positive and negative local and global impacts of the digital divide.

Safe and responsible practice

D-A

(a) Henry works at a computer most of the day. He eats lunch at his desk whilst reading emails.

Explain **two** ways these actions could put Henry's health and safety at risk. **(4 marks)**

⟩Guided⟩

1   It is unhealthy to sit at a desk all day without a

break because ....

....

> Read the question carefully. Think about the specific risks to Henry when he is eating his lunch at his PC and explain each point.

2   ....

....

E-C

(b) Give **two** precautions he could take to reduce the risk of back pain. **(2 marks)**

1   ....

....

2   ....

....

D-C

(c) Give **two** ways in which digital devices could cause a fire hazard. **(2 marks)**

1   ....

....

2   ....

....

D-A

(d) Explain **two** ways in which digital devices could improve Henry's health and well-being. **(4 marks)**

1   ....

....

2   ....

....

Sustainability issues

D-B

(a) Peter buys a new tablet computer. Peter recycles his old device.

State **two other** ways individuals can reduce the impact of ICT on the environment.

(2 marks)

Guided

1   You can keep using the device for as long as possible before replacing it.

2   ....

....

> Note the word 'other' in bold. Candidates often miss this word and write about the original statement, in this case recycling. Be sure to choose **two different** ways to answer the question fully.

C-A*

*(b) Discuss the environmental impact of ICT and how sustainability can be maximised.

(6 marks)

....

....

....

....

....

....

....

....

> This question has an asterisk which means that the quality of your written communication will be assessed. You need to think about your spelling, punctuation and grammar as well as clarity of expression. You need to give a balanced argument which considers both positive and negative effects and then explain them, ideally with examples. In questions like this one, students often forget to give any positive impacts.

....

....

....

....

....

....

....

....

....

....

Practice exam paper

Edexcel publishes official Sample Assessment Material on its website. This practice exam paper has been written to help you practise what you have learned and may not be representative of a real exam paper.

- Allow 1 hour and 30 minutes.
- Answer **all** questions.

Millie is a Year 10 student and is about to go on an exchange visit to Germany with her school.

She is a confident user of ICT. She uses ICT in learning, leisure and socialising.

Use this information to answer question 1(a).

Camera A		Camera B	
Image sensor	5 MP	Image sensor	12 MP
Optical zoom	No	Optical zoom	No
Digital zoom	Yes	Digital zoom	Yes
Removable storage	SD card	Removable storage	SD card
Battery life	3 hours	Battery life	5 hours
GPS	No	GPS	Yes
Connectivity	USB 2.0, Bluetooth	Connectivity	USB 3.0, HDMI, Bluetooth, Wi-Fi
Camera C		Camera D	
Image sensor	10 MP	Image sensor	3 MP
Optical zoom	Yes	Optical zoom	No
Digital zoom	Yes	Digital zoom	Yes
Removable storage	SD card	Removable storage	None
Battery life	5 hours	Battery life	2 hours
GPS	Yes	GPS	No
Connectivity	USB 2.0, Bluetooth, HDMI	Connectivity	USB 2.0

Some questions must be answered with a cross in a box ☒. If you change your mind about an answer, put a line through the box ☒ and then mark your new answer with a cross ☒.

1 Millie wants to buy a camera to take with her on the exchange visit.

(a) (i) Which camera will take the clearest pictures of distant objects? **(1)**

☐ Camera A

☐ Camera B

☐ Camera C

☐ Camera D

(ii) Which of these cameras has no wireless connectivity? **(1)**

☐ Camera A

☐ Camera B

☐ Camera C

☐ Camera D

(iii) Which camera can upload images directly to an online album? **(1)**

☐ Camera A

☐ Camera B

☐ Camera C

☐ Camera D

(iv) Which camera will produce the most suitable images for printing out poster-size pictures? **(1)**

☐ Camera A

☐ Camera B

☐ Camera C

☐ Camera D

(b) Some of Millie's friends are going to use their smartphones to take pictures on the trip.

Give **two** reasons why a digital camera might take clearer pictures than a smartphone. **(2)**

1 ....

....

2 ....

....

(c) Two of the cameras have GPS, allowing Millie to geotag her pictures.

(i) State what extra data is stored with the picture when it is geotagged. **(1)**

....

....

(ii) State why this is a useful feature. **(1)**

....

....

(iii) Millie's parents have advised her not to geotag the pictures that she uploads to her social networking site.

Explain why she should not do this. **(2)**

....

....

....

....

(d) Millie is going to upload her pictures to an online album.

Give **two** ways in which she will be able to control who can see the pictures. **(2)**

1 ....

....

2 ....

....

(Total for Question 1 = 12 marks)

2 Millie decides to buy her camera from an online shop.

(a) State **two** benefits to Millie of buying the camera online rather than from a high street shop. (2)

1 ....

....

2 ....

....

(b) State **one** possible drawback to Millie of buying the camera online rather than from a high street shop. (1)

....

....

(c) Many businesses now sell only on the Internet rather than having a high street shop.

List **two** benefits **to businesses** of selling goods this way. (2)

1 ....

....

2 ....

....

(d) The online shop stores Millie's personal details in their database.

(i) State **two** legal requirements they must meet when storing personal details in a database. (2)

1 ....

....

2 ....

....

(ii) Which law controls the information stored on customers? **(1)**

☐ **A** The Computer Misuse Act

☐ **B** The Retail Act

☐ **C** The Data Protection Act

☐ **D** The Copyright Act

(iii) Online shops display a statement on their websites about how they will use the data they gather.

> ▬ What information do we collect?
>
> Name, contact details, date of birth, credit card information, shopping selections, data about pages visited.
>
> ➕ How do we collect your personal information?
>
> ➕ What do we do with the information?

What is this statement called? **(1)**

☐ **A** Retail policy

☐ **B** Security policy

☐ **C** Online selling policy

☐ **D** Privacy policy

(e) State **two** ways that Millie can tell that the website is secure when she uses a bank card to pay for the camera. **(2)**

1 ....

....

2 ....

....

(f) When Millie bought the camera, the website automatically downloaded a small text file called a 'cookie' to her computer.

(i) State **one** benefit to Millie of receiving the cookie from the website. **(1)**

....

....

(ii) Give **two** reasons why Millie should consider deleting cookies from her computer. **(2)**

1 ....

....

2 ....

....

(Total for Question 2 = 14 marks)

3 Many of Millie's friends are using their smartphones for taking pictures, rather than carrying a digital camera.

(a) (i) When one electronic device develops new functions that were previously done by other devices, it is referred to as: **(1)**

☐ **A** Digital change

☐ **B** Divergence

☐ **C** Digital evolution

☐ **D** Convergence

(ii) State **two other** functions of smartphones that were previously carried out by other devices. **(2)**

1 ....

....

2 ....

....

(iii) Many devices, such as smartphones, are now 'multifunctional'.

Give **one other** example of a multifunctional device and state an extra function that it can now carry out. **(2)**

Multifunctional device:

....

Extra function:

....

(b) (i) When Millie and her friends arrive in Germany, they have a mobile phone signal from a local network.

Which **one** of the following allows them to use the local network? **(1)**

☐ **A** Broadband

☐ **B** Freeware

☐ **C** Roaming

☐ **D** Dial-up

(ii) They receive a welcome message from the network.

Which of the following would be used to send the message? **(1)**

☐ **A** SMS

☐ **B** GPS

☐ **C** MMS

☐ **D** HDMI

(c) Millie has also brought her Wi-Fi enabled laptop computer with her.

    (i)   Describe how she could transfer the pictures from her camera to her laptop.   **(2)**

....

....

....

    (ii) Millie backs up her pictures using the laptop's DVD drive.

          State **one other local** storage device, other than a CD or DVD drive, that could
be used for backups.   **(1)**

....

    (iii) Millie could also use online storage for her backups.

          Give **two** advantages of using online storage rather than DVD for backups.   **(2)**

      1 ....

....

      2 ....

....

(d) Millie is in an area with no Wi-Fi access.

(i) Describe how she could use her smartphone to allow her laptop to access
the Internet. **(2)**

....

....

....

(ii) State how Millie could prevent other devices from sharing the connection. **(1)**

....

....

(iii) Explain how sharing the connection might affect the uploading of the images. **(2)**

....

....

....

....

(Total for Question 3 = 17 marks)

4 While Millie is abroad she is keeping in touch with her friends at home.

One method she is using is a social networking site.

(a) (i) State what 'social networking' is. **(1)**

....

....

(ii) State **two** advantages to Millie of using a social networking site rather than voice calls to communicate with all of her friends at home. **(2)**

1 ....

....

2 ....

....

(iii) Some of Millie's friends exchange personal details with people who contact them on the social networking site.

Give **one** reason why they should not do this. **(1)**

....

....

(b) Using her laptop, Millie can make free voice calls to her friends at home over the Internet.

(i) Which protocol allows her to do this? **(1)**

☐ **A** HTTP

☐ **B** VoIP

☐ **C** IMAP

☐ **D** HTTPS

(ii) Millie finds that she cannot make these calls to some of her friends, even though they have computers.

List **two** items of hardware her friends will need in order to make these calls. **(2)**

1 ....

2 ....

(c) Millie also uses the Internet to email all of her friends at home.

Her mail program uses the IMAP protocol when she wants to read her emails.

(i) Explain how this protocol handles her emails differently from the POP protocol. **(2)**

....

....

....

....

(ii) State **one** benefit to Millie of using the IMAP protocol. **(1)**

....

....

(d) Millie also communicates with her friends at home using her blog.

She uploads pictures of her visit and writes about what she has been doing.

(i) If Millie uploads a picture that she has found on the Internet, she may be breaking which law? **(1)**

☐ **A** The Data protection Act

☐ **B** The Computer Misuse Act

☐ **C** The Copyright Act

☐ **D** The Computer Downloading Act

(ii) Millie tags her blog posts.

> Give your post a title
>
> River Cruise .
>
> Tags
>
> river, boat, sail, Bonn, Linz

Explain **one** benefit of using this feature. **(2)**

....

....

....

....

*(e) Discuss how the Internet has changed the way in which people's work and ideas can be published to a wide audience.

(6)

....

....

....

....

....

....

....

....

....

....

....

....

....

....

....

....

....

....

....

....

....

(Total for Question 4 = 19 marks)

5 While Millie and her friends are abroad, they can log into and use the school's VLE (Virtual Learning Environment).

  (a) (i) Describe how a VLE could be used to enhance the work they are doing on their trip.
                                                                                        (3)

  ....

  ....

  ....

  ....

    (ii) Millie has her own personal area on the school's VLE.
          List **two** ways in which she should be able to personalise her area.   (2)

    1 ....

       ....

    2 ....

       ....

  (b) Millie and her friends can access digital technology but many people are unable to.

    (i) The gap between people who can and cannot access digital technology is called: (1)

         ☐ **A** The social divide

         ☐ **B** The technology divide

         ☐ **C** The digital divide

         ☐ **D** The ICT divide

    (ii) Give **two** reasons why some people may not be able to access digital technology. (2)

    1 ....

       ....

    2 ....

       ....

    (iii) Describe the effects of a lack of digital access on people's lives.   (4)

  ....

  ....

  ....

  ....

*(c) The widespread use of the Internet has led to the creation of 'server farms' – large clusters of computers which store online data. It has been estimated that 'server farms' consume about 3% of the world's electricity supply.

Discuss the impact of the increasing use of digital devices on the environment and how we can improve sustainability.

(6)

....

....

....

....

....

....

....

....

....

....

....

....

....

....

....

....

....

....

....

(Total for Question 5 = 18 marks)

Answers

Personal digital devices

1. Uses of digital devices

(a) One of:

Use of specialist software results in greater productivity / more work being done.

People can work from home which saves money on transport / means lower carbon footprint.

People can access online data which allows people to collaborate on the same documents.

The use of video conferencing means that meetings can be organised quickly / you can have meetings with people all over the world / you save money on transport or accommodation.

(b) The following points would be valid in an answer to this question. Remember that the quality of your argument is important too.

Benefits of personal digital devices in education could include:

- Use of computers for producing and presenting work.
- Use of the Internet (on computers / tablets / mobile phones) for research.
- Subject-specific software for subject teaching.
- Use of digital projectors and interactive whiteboards in teaching.
- Use of various digital devices such as computers, smartphones and tablets for email communication.
- Use of various digital devices such as computers, smartphones and tablets with VLEs to allow effective communication among students, teachers and parents, to allow teachers to publish lesson content, and to allow students to hand in work.
- Use of educational apps on smartphones and tablets.
- Use of digital devices for datalogging.
- Use of digital cameras for projects, experiments and so on.

2. Using digital devices

The following points would be valid in an answer to this question. Remember that the quality of your argument is important too.

Economic

- Limited skills development and understanding of the use of technology.
- Limited awareness / skills can impact on jobs.
- more difficult to access banking and other online services.
- Goods cost more (it is often cheaper to buy goods / services online).
- Less choice (a wider range of options regarding goods / services online).

Social

- Digital exclusion.
- Poorer online (less immediate) access to email / other communications (also applies to mobile phones, and so on, not just broadband).

- Exclusion (opportunity to link into social networking / developing friendship / common interest groups).
- Poorer access to 'now' society (immediate contact / access to news).

Educational

- Poorer access to information (many educational resources now freely available online) and online courses.
- No access to online training (would need to access community resources and would have to leave home to do this).
- Limited opportunity to develop skills (ICT and other functional skills).

Cultural

- Poorer access to resources such as:
- Music (MP3 and MP4 players / downloads / streaming).
- Video on demand (BBC iPlayer and similar).

3. Common features

(a) D All of them.

(b) (i) 1 A hard disk drive has greater storage capacity.

2 Faster data access.

(ii) Any **two** from:

- SD card is smaller and lighter.
- No moving parts that can be damaged.
- Easily removable and can be used to transfer data between devices.

4. Input and output devices

(a) One of:

- Inbuilt webcam cannot be lost.
- Inbuilt webcam means there are no additional cables.
- No need to install additional software / no set up time required.
- An inbuilt webcam is less likely to get damaged than an external one.

(b) One of:

- Provides better clarity / excludes outside noise / noise cancellation.
- Means that she has her hands free enabling her to take notes or perform other tasks.
- Less distracting for other people in the vicinity.

(c) Tablet computer C

(d) One of:

- Allows him to display two files side by side so he can work on them at the same time.
- Gives him a higher resolution screen.
- Allows easier sharing of laptop information with other users (assuming laptop screen is small).

5. Connectivity

(a) 1 Wi-Fi

2 Bluetooth

(b) (i) Synchronisation means keeping multiple copies of files on different devices identical: if one is changed it will automatically be changed on the other device. If she downloads a file to her laptop it will automatically be transferred to her media player and smartphone or if she changes contact details on one device they will be changed on the others.

(ii) Any **two** from:

- To fix or patch bugs.
- To add new features / functionality.
- To improve performance / functionality / user interface (UI).

(c) Items she downloads will be saved online (in the cloud) and will automatically be available to all of her devices using Wi-Fi / she will not have to connect the devices for them to synchronise.

6. Mobile phones 1

(a) Mobile phone B

(b) Mobile phone A

(c) One of:

- Wi-Fi.
- GPS.
- GPRS.
- EDGE.
- WAP-enabled.
- Web browser.

(d) Any **two** from:

- Using a sat nav app on your mobile phone, GPS can help you find your way by giving directions from current location to destination.
- Gives current location / finding out where you are / locate me.
- Gives distance from current location to specified location.
- Gives estimated time from current location to specified location.
- Gives location of key services, for example nearest train station or ATM.
- Allows users to tag images / locations of interest to other mobile phone users.

7. Mobile phones 2

(a) Any **two** from:

- Set a PIN.
- Password protect.
- Lock SIM card.
- Encrypt data.

(b) B the countries in which the phone can be used

(c) (i) Any **two** from:

- Large memory for storing music and videos.
- High resolution camera with video.
- Ability to download and stream movies.
- High resolution screen.

(ii) HDMI lead.

(iii) One of:

- Docking station.
- Wi-Fi speakers.

(d) One of:

- Accidents by texting while walking down busy streets.
- Radiation by long exposure to phone calls may cause damage to brain.
- RSI injuries.

8. Personal computers 1

(a) Tablet computer C

(b) Any **two** from:

- Rotating the screen from landscape to portrait depending on which way you are holding the tablet.
- Controlling apps (for example compass, music player, crash sensors, shake feature and so on).
- Controlling or playing games.
- Image stabilisation.
- To turn the device on.

(c) C 3G

(d) One of:

- Higher quality / more detail in the image.
- A clearer image / picture.
- More vertical and horizontal pixel lines.
- More pixels per inch^2 / cm^2 / dpi.

(e) One of:

- Possible RSI.
- Eye strain.
- Finger stress / pressure on fingers.

9. Personal computers 2

(a) Any **two** from:

- The processor: the quicker the **processor speed**, the faster your device will work.
- Amount of memory: the more **RAM** it has, the more applications it will be able to support.
- Hard disk size: the more **storage capacity** you have, the more files you can save.
- Sound / graphics card: the **sound / graphics** card is important if you use a lot of graphics, videos, music or games.
- Wi-Fi enabled: can access home networks and Internet.
- Communications ports: HDMI for connection to HD television / number of USB ports for connecting peripherals.

(b) C Ergonomics

(c) One of:

- Incorrect seating position.
- Sitting in the same position for too long.

(d) Any **two** from:

Risk 1 Eye strain from looking at a screen for too long or light falling on the monitor.

One solution from:

- Take regular breaks away from screen.
- Move the screen so that it is not reflecting light directly.
- Use an antiglare screen.

Risk 2 Repetitive strain injury from repeated movements.

One solution from:

- Use wrist rests to support hands.
- Take breaks from repeating actions.
- Don't use the same input device all the time.

10. Cameras and camcorders 1

(a) Camcorder D

(b) (i) It is waterproof and shockproof.

(ii) Memory card / SD card.

(c) Camcorder C

(d) **One** of:

- To preview / review the footage.
- To see what is being recorded.
- To view / use the menu.
- So that the viewfinder does not have to be used.

11. Cameras and camcorders 2

(a) **D** GPS

(b) **A** Wi-Fi

(c) They will be able to copy the coordinates and paste them into online maps for example Google Maps or Google Earth. The maps will show them exactly where they were taken and Google Earth will show pictures of the area.

(d) She could set the albums as private and send emails to invite friends to view them set access rights to the albums.

12. Media players 1

(a) Personal media player D

(b) Any **two** from:

- Set a password / code / pin / security pattern / biometrics.
- Lock the device manually OR automatically after a certain length of time / inactivity.
- Deactivate / password protect / hide the Bluetooth / wireless sharing.
- Remote management (deactivation).
- Hard reset feature (to protect data if device sold / disposed of).
- Encryption (of data).
- Antivirus.
- Backup features.

(c) Any **two** from:

- Headphones / earphones.
- Speakers.
- Docking station.
- Remote control.
- FM receiver / transmitter.
- Bluetooth receiver / transmitter.
- GPS receiver.
- Fitness sensor.
- Camera.

(d) 1 MPEG-4.

2 WMV.

(e) **D** HDMI

13. Media players 2

(a) (i) The MP3 format uses less data to store the audio information which means that MP3 files are quick to download.

OR

MP3 is a popular format which increases compatibility.

(ii) Reduced audio / sound quality.

(iii) **One** of:

- It is illegal to make a copy of software / it is illegal to copy software and make money.
- Copyright, Designs and Patents Act.

(b) (i) Any **two** from:

- Does not use as much storage space.
- No need to wait for file to download before watching video / downloading takes longer / (streaming) saves time.
- Allows user to watch live / real time video.

(ii) Any **two** from:

- Video is not available to watch offline.
- Cannot keep (own) a local copy.
- Cannot watch if Internet connection unavailable.
- Limited availability for some streamed video.
- User experience is dependent on connection quality / playback might be affected by buffering / video might lag / video might freeze.

14. Games consoles 1

(a) (i) **One** of:

- HD TV.
- HDMI cable.
- HD cable.

(ii) Any **two** from:

- Consoles do not require much set up compared with PCs.
- Consoles come with ready-made controllers.
- You can play on a console without having to set it up on a desk.
- Consoles are compact – you do not need extra peripherals for gaming.
- Consoles are designed specifically for gaming.
- You can play hands free on a console.
- The newest gaming technology and games are always available on consoles first.

(iii) Any **three** from:

- Wireless controller.
- Wireless headset.
- Hard disk drive and transfer cable.
- Webcam, speaker and headphone set.
- Hands-free gaming kit.
- Balance board.

(b) Any **two** from:

- Access the Internet.
- Playing CD, DVD, Blu-ray / watching videos / listening to music.

- Social networking.
- Stream / download video / music.

(c) (i) **One** of:

- It might be harder to copy (to a disk) an electronic download of a game.
- They can track where an illegal copy of a game might have come from.
- Wider audience for the product / more ways to buy.
- Saves money on CDs / cheaper to produce / distribution costs.
- Helps environmental targets / eco-credentials of the company.
- Collection of marketing data.

(ii) **One** of:

- Carbon footprint will be reduced because less power / fewer resources used to create disk and packaging.
- Lower emissions from transport / distribution.
- Less waste produced meaning less landfill / recycling costs.

15. Games consoles 2

(a) Any **two** from:

- Make sure the screen is adjusted properly for contrast and brightness
- Take frequent 'gaze' breaks, such as looking at distant objects to change the focal point.
- Rearrange the furniture so that any light source, such as a window, does not shine into your face or onto the monitor.

(b) If Emma spends most of her free time playing games then there's a good chance she'll start to fall behind with school work and her grades could slip. She could end up isolated from her real friends if she spends all of her time gaming with virtual friends. Also, she's in danger of finding herself with no other hobbies or interests which would look bad on job or university applications.

(c) 1 Can lead to aggression.

2 Can decrease empathy for others.

3 Can affect emotional control.

16. Home entertainment systems

(a) (i) To transform the signal from the cable or satellite to a form that can be used by the television.

(ii) Pause / rewind the programme.

(iii) **One** of:

- Broadband.
- Internet.
- Telephone.

(b) They could connect the Blu-ray player to the TV using HDMI. They would set up a home Wi-Fi network. They could then stream the sound from the TV to the speakers using Wi-Fi.

17. Satellite navigation 1

(a) (i) To provide an accurate location / tell you where you are.

(ii) **One** of:

- It saves Shameela time because she does not need to enter the address again.
- It saves the geodata with a user-friendly name so Shameela can recall it more easily later.

(iii) Any **two** from:

- Distractions, stress or lack of understanding of device may cause an accident / stress.
- Incorrect positioning of device may cause a blind spot / affect visibility.
- Driver may take eyes off road to look at the screen and not see cars and pedestrians.

(b) Any **two** from:

- Can deal with unexpected incidents / provide alternative routes.
- Provide traffic updates.
- Plot speed.
- Give estimated arrival time.
- Calculate current distance to destination.
- Can map petrol stations / motorway services on your route.
- Get live traffic reports.
- Warn of speed cameras.
- Provide details and images of places of interest on the route.

18. Satellite navigation 2

(a) **One** of:

- They provide information about where to locate disabled parking areas.
- They provide local information about disabled facilities at shops, rail stations and toilets.

(b) 1 You only have to have one device with you (you do not need a separate sat nav).

2 People tend to leave sat navs in their cars, which is a security risk, whereas they tend not to leave their mobile phones in their cars.

(c) You can connect your mobile phone and the sat nav using Bluetooth so that the sat nav (which has inbuilt speakers and microphone) acts as the hands free allowing drivers to make calls safely.

19. Impact on organisations

The following points would be valid in an answer to this question. Remember that the quality of your argument is important too.

Employees:

- Mobile phones allow workers to communicate with each other and with customers anywhere and at any time.
- Laptops, netbooks and tablets allow people to work away from the office, when they are travelling or when at home. More people can work from home and not commute.
- Greater collaboration between workers at different sites.

- Wi-Fi and 3G networks allow workers to access an organisation's files and data from anywhere in the world using portable digital devices and organisation's data can be stored in the 'cloud' so all employees can access it.

- More online work and communication means that organisations must concentrate on security to prevent hackers stealing or corrupting data.

- As more employees have digital devices of their own more organisations support corporate applications on employee-owned devices such as notebooks, smartphones and tablets. This is difficult to manage because of the different types of devices and security concerns.

Customers:

- As more of their customers use portable digital devices, organisations must cater for them by:
  ○ creating websites – to showcase what they do
  ○ selling online – more convenient for customers
  ○ creating blogs – many organisations use blogs to tell customers about developments in a more personal way
  ○ social networking – most organisations have a presence on social networking sites / they monitor comments and communications and engage in two-way discussions.

- Two-way communication with customers and potential customers is critical to the success of a business.

Connectivity

20. Home networks

(a) Any **two** from:
- Backing up data to another computer.
- Sharing files on each other's computers.
- Sharing a printer.
- Sharing an Internet connection.

(b) Router

(c) (i) Any **two** from:
- They do not have to run cables all over the house.
- They do not have to install plugs / access points in all of the rooms.
- They can connect anywhere in the house.
- They can move from room to room with a device and remain connected.

(ii) **One** of:
- If they are too far away from the router they will not get a wireless signal.
- If there are other electrical devices nearby they may get interference.
- If there is an obstruction / wall / and so on this may block the signal.

(d) The film they want to watch is HD which means they will need more bandwidth to view it. A cable connection offers much higher bandwidth than a Wi-Fi connection.

21. Network security

(a) The network is unsecured which means that it is viewable by anyone and therefore any device can connect to their wireless signal.

(b) (i) **One** of:
- He could disable Service Set Identifier (SSID) broadcasting.
- The router broadcasts the name of the network at regular intervals. This could be turned off so computers are not aware of it.

(ii) Find out MAC address of each device on his network and only allow those devices onto the wireless network.

(c) (i) A form of encryption (must use the word 'encryption').

(ii) WPA encrypts or scrambles messages sent over the network so that they cannot be read by anyone who does not have the encryption key.

22. Combining technologies

(a) **One** of:
- Ryan could set up his phone as a router / hotspot and use Wi-Fi.
- Ryan could pair / connect / link the devices using Wi-Fi.

(b) **One** of:
- Set an access key / password / PIN.
- Block unknown devices (IP / MAC filtering).
- Make sure device is not within range of other devices.
- Turn Wi-Fi off.
- Hide SSID.

(c) As more devices use the connection, the available bandwidth is reduced / less / divided.

23. Bandwidth and latency

(a) Low latency will improve her gaming experience because she is playing online and needs to transmit data as quickly as possible to the server and other players.

(b) **C** 30 megabits per second

(c) As her bandwidth is shared with other Internet users there may be contention / reduction in bandwidth depending on how many other users are connected.

(d) If you are downloading a lot of files at the same time, there will be a lot of bits going through the network. This can cause the network to perform more slowly than usual.

24. Wi-Fi and mobile broadband

(a) (i) **B** Hotspots

(ii) Hackers can set up open networks and can obtain passwords and financial information from users who connect.

(b) (i) **C** Mobile broadband

(ii) Benefits:
1 3G provides far greater coverage than Wi-Fi
2 3G is more secure because all data is encrypted.

Any **two** drawbacks from:
- 3G has lower bandwidth than Wi-Fi.

- You always have to pay to use 3G.
- When using abroad you incur roaming charges.
- When using 3G you may have download limits.

25. Peer-to-peer networks

(a) (i) **One** of:
  - No access point is needed.
  - The devices can connect directly to each other.

(ii) 1 USB Cable

   2 Transfer SD card from mobile to laptop.

(b) Wi-Fi has a longer range. It also offers higher bandwidth and transmission speed.

26. Communication protocols 1

(a) **B** VoIP

(b) 1 Microphone.

   2 Speakers.

(c) SMTP

(d) (i) Benefit:

   IMAP allows Katerina to access her inbox from any location on the network using different devices.

   One drawback of:
  - You need an Internet connection to be able to access your emails on the server – cannot read offline.
  - The mail server might get full and Katerina will have to increase space available or delete old messages.
  - You can get synchronisation conflicts if you change something on your server and on your local copy.

(ii) Unlike IMAP, POP downloads emails from the mail server to a computer. The emails are then deleted from the mail server and users read the emails offline.

27. Communication protocols 2

(a) HTTP

(b) (i) **One** of:
  - The URL should change from http:// to https://.
  - Padlock symbol (browser-dependent).

(ii) Digital certificates are issued by an authentication company to certify the identity of the server you are attached to and when it was last inspected.

(c) The data that is sent is scrambled or encoded. Only the server and your computer can decode it using the encryption key that they have agreed on.

28. Security risks in a network

(a) (i) He may not have updated the antivirus software / downloaded updates.

(ii) A firewall is used to stop (or allow) data transmission between his computer and others on the Internet to stop malicious sites from downloading malware and accessing data on his computer.

(iii) Any **two** from:

- He should try to avoid file-sharing websites.
- Do not download from unknown websites.
- Do not open email attachments from unknown senders.

(b) Any **two** from:
  - Use letters and numbers in a password.
  - Use upper and lower case characters in a password.
  - Use punctuation marks in a password.
  - Do not use whole words as passwords because they are easier to guess.

29. Physical security risks

The following points would be valid in an answer to this question. Remember that the quality of your argument is important too.

To prevent illegal access and theft of hardware:

- All doors should be locked and fitted with security keypads.
- Burglar alarms should be fitted in all rooms.
- Closed circuit television cameras should be placed inside and outside the building so all areas can be continually scanned.
- Security chains on computers and peripherals to lock them to desks.
- Security marking on hardware, for example postcode written by UV pen.
- RFID chips in hardware to sound alarm if taken through a scanner.

Authentication of staff to prevent illegal access to hardware and data:

- Login names and passwords.
- Use of swipe cards to authenticate identity when entering room – could be lost or stolen.
- Biometric methods of identification – finger prints scanning, iris recognition and voice recognition.
- Audit trails to monitor all network use.

Operating online

30. The Internet

(a) **C** HTTP

(b) NIC / Network Interface Card.

(c) (i) Any **three** explanatory points, such as:

- It offers high bandwidth which the family will need for streaming and playing online games.
- It offers enough email addresses for the whole family.
- It offers parental controls which will allow Mr and Mrs Smith to protect their children.
- It offers unlimited download so the family will not be charged for all their downloading and streaming.

(ii) A firewall blocks connections between computers on the network and your own. You can set the rules about which computers can communicate with yours and the software on your computer that can access the Internet. This prevents hackers from installing malware on your computer.

31. Internet use 1

(a) 3G / mobile Internet.

(b) A blog is a shared online diary. People use blogs to share details of their experiences and to publish photos. Other people can read the entries and comment on them.

(c) Any **two** from:

- It is cheaper to upload to social networking site because she does not have to pay for messages.
- She can reach all her friends with one upload rather than sending multiple messages.
- Her friends can comment on her photo uploads for all friends to see.

(d) 1 Set the albums as private rather than public.

2 Give access rights for different people to be able to view them and / or edit them.

(e) (i) VoIP / Voice over Internet Protocol.

(ii) There is not enough bandwidth because of other users downloading or using the Internet.

32. Internet use 2

(a) (i) Any **two** from:

- Better than conference calls because you can see who you are talking to and their body language.
- Employees do not have to travel long distances to meetings.
- Allows companies to work more easily with people all over the world.
- Lower travel and accommodation costs saves the company money.

(ii) Any **two** from:

- If the computers crash or the equipment fails, the meeting might have to be rescheduled.
- People need extra training.
- People needed to maintain and set up equipment.
- People communicate better if they are all in the same room.

(b) The Internet has made it much easier for students to carry out research and find information from specialist websites. Online applications, email and instant messaging allow students to collaborate with each other more easily and they can also use wikis to share ideas.

33. Security measures

(a) (i) **B** C-hor4se

(ii) This is to check that Sereena typed her password correctly the first time she entered it.

(iii) She might share her computer with others and this makes it possible for someone else to use her account without her permission.

(b) To provide an additional layer of security and so that she can access her account if she forgets her password.

(c) **B** prevent automated sign-up scripts.

34. Personal spaces

(a) Any **three** from:

- Teachers can publish detailed lesson information that students can access online at school, at home or when on holiday.
- Teachers can use it to provide feedback to students.
- It can provide links to useful sources of information.
- Courses can be personalised for individual students.
- Students can hand in homework and teachers can mark it and provide feedback online.
- It can have online tests for students and store their scores.
- Parents can view student grades, attendance, test results and check progress.
- Parents can use it to communicate with teachers.
- Students can collaborate on projects.
- Students can request help and contribute to forums and notice boards.
- It can be used for polls and questionnaires to poll student and parent views.

(b) 1 He could add text, such as a profile of himself.

2 He could add weblinks and news feeds.

(c) Any **two** from:

- Not post anything online that he would not want to make public.
- Minimising details that disclose his address or whereabouts.
- Keeping account numbers, user names and passwords secret.
- Only sharing his email address with people he knows.
- Not use apps that use GPS to share his location with others.

(d) James should act quickly by getting in touch with the forum administrator and asking for the offensive message to be removed.

35. Information misuse

(a) Any **two** from:

- name
- address
- gender
- email address.

(b) To enhance security / protect Jane's personal information / protect payment information / stop information being read by people who could be looking at the screen.

(c) Spyware

(d) Most computer security software is very strong so hackers and criminals rely on tricking people to install malware. They do this by making fake sites or software that encourage people to install the malware without knowing they have done so.

36. Preventing misuse

(a) Cookies

(b) Any **two** from:
- What information the company is gathering about you.
- How the company gathers information about you.
- How the company will use the information they gather about you.
- Whether the company intends to pass your information on to others.
- How the company. securely stores your information.
- How you can access the data held about you.

(c) Any **two** from:
- Use a firewall to prevent spyware from being remotely downloaded to your computer by hackers.
- Install antispyware protection software which removes or blocks spyware.
- Only download programs from websites you trust.
- Read all security warnings, license agreements and privacy statements.
- Never click 'agree' or 'OK' to close a window. Instead, click the red 'x' in the corner of the window.
- Be wary of popular 'free' music and movie file-sharing programs.

(d) (i) **C** phishing
(ii) Any **two** from:
- Impersonal greeting: 'Dear Customer' – does not address you by name.
- There is a sense of urgency: 'we urgently need you'.
- Strict time limit imposed: 'within the next 36 hours.
- Threat: 'terminate your account'.
- The URL starts with http rather than https.

37. Legislation

(a) (i) Any **two** from:
- Digital files can be copied more easily than paper files.
- Hard to tell if data has been changed, with no crossing out and so on.
- Easier to steal – do not have to carry away lots of files.
- Can steal data online – do not have to physically break into an office.

(ii) Data Protection Act
(iii) Any **two** from:
- Control entry to the building so that only authorised people can physically access the database.
- Encrypt the data so that it cannot be read.
- Install a firewall to prevent unauthorised remote access.
- Keep a log of who accesses the data so that this can be audited to detect unauthorised access.

- Makes users login and enter a password so that only authorised users can access the database.

(iv) Any **two** from:
- She has the right to look at and check the data held but they can charge her for this.
- She can demand that incorrect information is amended.
- She can demand that the data is not used in any way that could harm or distress her.
- She can demand that her data is not used for direct marketing.

(b) The Computer Misuse Act was introduced due to hackers / criminals. It allows the government to prosecute people who access computers and steal or change data without permission.

38. Copyright

(a) Music is expensive to produce – instruments, recording equipment, time and so on. If the people who produce it do not get any money they will stop making good quality music and the Internet will be full of second rate music files to download. If musicians cannot earn money, then they will stop producing music and people in the industry will be made redundant.

(b) **C** The Copyright, Designs and Patents Act

(c) Any **two** from:
- Musicians do not need a record company to be able to produce and sell music.
- It is cheaper to record and distribute music digitally.
- Musicians can do all recording and selling themselves.
- There are online music communities and online music stores that allow musicians to promote their music.

(d) (i) She must not use images without permission of the copyright holder / owner because she would be breaching Copyright.

OR

She must not use images without permission of the copyright holder / owner to protect intellectual property rights.

(ii) She would need to apply to the copyright owner for permission to reproduce the images in her book. She may have to pay to use them and will have to acknowledge the copyright owner in her book.

Online goods and services

39. Online shopping 1

(a) (i) **D** Some services and goods are now only available for purchase online.

(ii) Any **two** from:
- He will be able to read other customers' reviews.
- He will be able to search / sort for the records.
- He will be able to listen to parts of the tracks.

(b) Any **two** from:

- Facility to search for train / cheapest train.
- Facility to pay for the ticket online.
- Facility to make seat reservation for a particular seat.
- Facility to see timetable and calculate arrival times.
- Online account is held about him so he does not have to key in his details again and which may have remembered his preferences from previous journeys.

(c) Explanation to include any **three** from:

- People can shop from home at high street shops or online-only shops.
- It is much easier to buy things from all over the world.
- People research their purchases by comparing different products, services and prices.
- Individual people may buy easily from other individuals using auction websites.
- People have changed the main way they pay for items: credit cards and third parties such as PayPal are used much more because they are accepted online.
- People visit high street stores less, so these may be in decline.
- People buy more 'virtual' products because they are easier to buy online.

40. Online shopping 2

(a) (i) Any **two** from:

- She is able to search and sort through more items more quickly.
- She can shop for clothes 24/7/365.
- She does not need to leave her home to purchase the dress.
- She can read customer reviews of the dress.
- She can compare the price the dress is being sold at on different websites.

(ii) Any **two** from:

- She cannot try the dress on. / The dress may be the wrong size.
- The dress may not be what she wants when it arrives.
- She cannot touch and feel the dress.
- The photo and description may be misleading.
- She has to wait for the dress to arrive before she can wear it.
- She may have to return the dress.

(b) Catherine has the right to return the dress up to 7 days after receiving it. She is entitled to a full refund.

(c) (i) Any **two** from:

- He will have lower overheads (less staff and lower rent).
- Operating online is a good way to reach new markets.
- He can base his business wherever he likes.
- He will find it easier to make changes to products and prices.

(ii) **One** of:

- Older people who find it difficult to get to the shops.
- People with an illness or a disability who find high street shopping difficult.
- People who live in remote areas and have to travel a long way to high street shops.

41. Online auctions

(a) (i) First of all, Paul would need to create an online account with the auction website. Then, he can list his revision notes for sale giving a description / a photo / assigning a category.

(ii) **One** of:

- More potential buyers.
- Auction means that he will get the highest possible price.
- Can sell them from home – more convenient.

(b) **One** of:

- Online auction websites often use third party payment processors. This means that Paul's credit card details will not be shared with the seller, so they will be protected.
- If the football cards are rare, it is likely that not many high street stores will stock them. An online auction has many sellers from many countries so he is more likely to be able to find the cards.
- Online auctions have many sellers all competing for business, which will drive down prices.

42. Online education, news and banking

The following points would be raised in an answer to this question. Remember that the quality of your argument is important too.

Positives:

- Gives more people a voice / more people can publish – more freedom of speech.
- Increased availability of information.
- Increase in choice of service providers (locally and globally).
- News stories can break more quickly.
- Relative small cost lowers participation barrier.
- Competition drives traditional publishers to innovate with their provision of online content.
- News becomes interactive.
- News can be accessed based on personal preference.
- Readers can share articles with networks of friends.
- Stories / information popularised by public, not editors.
- Edemocracy – information is made available to and / or from politically 'sensitive' areas.
- WikiLeaks-style anonymity increases accountability (of governments and so on).

Negatives:

- More people can publish – dilution of content / lack of credibility.
- More difficult to filter content (students may describe this as 'information overload').
- News sensationalised by public, not editors.

- More difficult to track publishers of sensitive / libellous material.
- Limits frame of reference.
- Intellectual property rights of traditional publishers is put at risk.

43. Online gaming and entertainment

(a) Any **two** from:
- Available on mobile devices.
- Search and sort the entertainment media.
- Pause, play, fast forward and rewind.

(b) Streaming the data means she is able to watch it as soon as enough data is stored, while the rest of the data is being downloaded. It is stored temporarily to Kate's computer and she cannot watch it offline.

Downloading means all the data must be downloaded before she can watch the programme. She can watch it offline.

(c) The TV programme might stop playing as it waits for more information to be streamed over the Internet.

44. How and why organisations operate online

(a) **One** of:
- Andrew will need a secure online payment system.
- Andrew will need skilled staff to develop and run the website.
- He will need a delivery service.
- Online advertising may be expensive.
- Excludes customers without Internet access.

(b) **One** of:
- Does not need to pay for a shop.
- Only needs a website.
- Customers only need a web browser and Internet connection to buy his products.
- Location is not important.

(c) An online shop can be run from home or from cheaper premises because customers do not need to visit the physical location: there is less rent to pay. There is generally less need for assistants in online shops, so lower wages to be paid. The product is the same, therefore the overheads are lower, and so more of the selling price is profit.

(d) **One** of:
- A cheap way to expand.
- A way to reach customers who are not local.

45. Transactional data

(a) Any **two** from:
- Date and time of purchase.
- A unique reference number.
- A list of the items purchased.
- Tracking data that displays delivery status and location.
- Personal information from her online account.

(b) Any **two** from:
- She can track her delivery.

- She may be offered a more personalised experience on the website that is based on her past purchases.
- She may receive emails with special offers on items she is interested in.
- Her personal details will be stored so she does not have to keep typing them in.
- She can look at her order history and possibly track returns.

(c) Collecting transactional data (information about online purchases) has had many positive effects on organisations. It gives them lots of information about their customers, it can help them identify sales trends and it allows them to create targeted advertising campaigns. However, it's not all good news because organisations have had to spend a lot of money on systems to keep this data secure.

46. Internet advertising 1

(a) **One** of:
- It can be targeted at particular customers, so make them more likely to respond.
- It is cheaper than TV adverts, so saves money.
- It reaches a wide range of customers because it can be seen constantly through the advertising period, not just for 15 seconds at the end of a programme.
- It reaches customers much faster than traditional advertising because it can be put live immediately it is ready.

(b) Search engine advertisements work by displaying adverts when users type relevant key words into the search engine. *EasyFly* could carefully choose key words such as 'cheap flights' and create a relevant advertisement with a link to their website. Because the advert is something the user is interested in, he or she is more likely to click on it. *EasyFly* will only pay when a user clicks on the link.

(c) A large social network such as Facebook has millions of users who have uploaded lots of personal information, and this allows Facebook to target users based on factors such as gender, location, age and general interests.

47. Internet advertising 2

(a) **One** of:
- Spreads rapidly.
- Memorable content.

(b) **One** of:
- They do not need to pay for the adverts to be aired as they are spread 'virally'.
- By creating memorable content it is likely many more people will know about the group.
- They can create adverts where people can see and hear the band, so will know if they like it.

(c) MixUp could collect and combine online data from transactional data, social networking sites, microblogging sites, mobile phone apps and viral marketing to identify possible customers for its products. They could then send adverts to these users using social networking sites, email and content websites.

48. Internet advertising 3

(a) Any **two** from:

- The website could compile 'favourites' for Martin based on his interests.
- The website could recommend items for Martin based on analysis of his past purchases.
- The website could show Martin items he has recently viewed by listing his recently browsed web pages.
- The website could let Martin set up email reminders for special occasions such as birthdays.

(b) 1 Martin will see special offers that are likely to interest him.

2 Products that are likely to interest him will be featured, saving him time searching for them.

(c) **One** of:

- He may find it annoying.
- He may find it an invasion of his privacy, as it is based on his earlier purchases / browsing history.
- He may have placed previous orders on behalf of a friend, so the ads will be irrelevant to him.

(d) Any **two** from:

- Delete his cookies. / Change his privacy settings.
- Be careful what personal information he gives.
- If the data has come from another organisation, Martin could opt out of sharing his information with other organisations.

49. Payment systems 1

(a) C

(b) Entering the CCV means the person entering the code must have seen the credit card.

(c) Any **two** from:

- The URL changes from http: to https (s stands for secure).
- A padlock symbol is displayed.
- The colour of the address bar has changed.
- Use sites offering Verisign which adds a further layer of authentication.

(d) Secure Sockets Layer is a means of encrypting data (in this case from his credit card) to protect his details when they are transferred over the Internet.

50. Payment systems 2

(a) Any **two** from:

- The bank will check his account doesn't show any unusual activity.
- Login protection schemes such as PINsentry machine.
- Secure encrypted services.

(b) (i) **One** of:

- Credit / debit card details are not given to the selling organisation.
- Can buy from websites that do not offer https.
- Protection against unauthorised use of payment details.
- Protection if an item goes missing.
- The service is free to Abdul.

(ii) **One** of:

- Does not have to provide SSL which can be expensive.
- They will have more potential buyers as many people only pay online using a third party payment processor such as PayPal.

(c) Any **two** from:

- Security due to short transmission range.
- Security from limited applications – losing an NFC card loses only the credit on that card.
- Instant payments just by waving card over reader – great for busy shops.

51. Consumer protection

(a) She has the same rights as in a high street shop, so she can return the T-shirt and ask for a refund because it is faulty.

(b) Only websites belonging to companies located in the UK are subject to the UK consumer protection laws, so the cooling off period does not apply. Therefore it will depend on the laws of the country where the website is based.

(c) The 'cooling off period' for Internet purchases does not apply to perishable items such as flowers.

(d) Any **two** from:

- They can return faulty goods.
- They have a cooling off period in which they can change their mind.
- Reputable companies have privacy policies to protect data collected.
- Reputable websites encrypt payment details.
- Need to log into account providing a level of security.
- Third party payment processors guarantee security of payment details.

52. Applications software

(a) (i) Hosted software runs on a remote computer accessed over a network.

(ii) 1 It can be accessed from anywhere with Internet access and a web browser.

2 It doesn't take up much file space on your computer's hard disk drive.

(iii) Any **two** from:

- It cannot work without Internet access.
- The software is not as secure as the hosting company may be targeted by hackers.
- Response time depends on network speed.

(b) 1 Comparison websites.

2 Blogs which review the software.

3 He could discuss the software in online chat rooms.

(c) (i) Open source software has been produced by groups of people who believe that software and source code should be available for free to everyone.

(ii) **One** of:

- Jack does not have to pay for the software licence.
- Jack can access and modify the source code used to write the software.

(iii) One of:

- It may not be as feature-rich as proprietary software.
- There is no guarantee that problems / bugs will be fixed.
- Jack may need to learn new skills to use it.
- Jack may not be able to use his existing files and templates.

53. Commercial response to SaaS

(a) Any **two** from:

- Contains applications such as a word processor or spreadsheet in a browser.
- The applications are accessed over the Internet.
- The software is not installed on your local computer.

(b) One of:

- Make their products more appealing and better quality with more facilities and functions.
- Provide software 'bundled' in when you buy a computer.
- Provide technical support, help services and training materials.
- Use copyright to protect their products to stop similar 'free' products being offered as a 'software service'.

54. Storage: local or online?

(a) Any **two** from:

- Data is available anywhere you have Internet access and a browser.
- Easy to share data with others.
- Data is backed up for you.

(b) Any **two** from:

- Jason has less control of his data as he does not know where it is stored.
- He has to trust that the organisation storing his data will keep it secure.
- The online data storage may not be reliable.
- Needs an Internet connection to get access to his data. This can be frustrating if the connection is slow.

(c) Larger capacity of a DVD.

55. Search engines

(a) Any **two** from:

- Summaries seem relevant.
- Reputable websites.
- Well worded.
- No spelling mistakes.
- Norton OK symbol.
- Is it up to date, check preview to see if it is full of advertising.

(b) As anyone can contribute to the Wiki without their contribution being checked, their views might be biased or inaccurate.

(c) Result B is an Internet ad and a company has paid for it to appear at the top of the page when certain key words, including 'earthquakes', are searched for.

(d) Any **two** from:

- Add more key words to narrow down the search.
- Search by the type of object you are searching, for example image, a webpage, news, maps or videos.
- Use the advanced search facilities of the search engine.
- Use different types of search to gain more specific results, for example Earthquake AND Africa.

Online communities

56. Online communities – what are they?

(a) Any **two** from:

- She only has to post one message to reach all her friends rather than sending lots of different ones.
- Allows chat (real-time conversation).
- SMS requires payment for each person receiving message.
- Can send message without mobile phone signal / with Internet connection.
- Can add metadata (such as geodata).
- People can comment on / discuss the message.
- Can add multimedia to the message.

(b) Any **two** from:

- Online work spaces.
- Social bookmarking.
- User-generated reference sites.

(c) The functions and target audiences of each are different, so the features are tailored to those. Social networking is about friends updating each other on their lives at any time and wherever they are in the world, so profiles, images, videos, updates and timelines are very important and key features tend to be centred on those. VLEs are focused on education and communication within one organisation. Therefore features such as timetables, homework submission and communication with a teacher or tutor are important.

57. Online workspaces and VLEs

(a) (i) Any **two** from:

- Shared folders and files.
- Email and chat.
- Online conferencing (including virtual whiteboards).
- Online applications (such as word processors and spreadsheets).

(ii) One from:

- They can see versions of the documents, so they know which is the latest.
- Everything is kept in one place, so easy to find.
- It is available to them wherever they have an Internet connection.
- They can make it available easily to other people to review.
- They can set levels of access to the files to protect them.

(b) (i) Any **two** from:
- Teachers can put up detailed information about the lessons.
- Marking tools for the teachers.
- Allows teachers to track progress.
- New feeds (RSS).
- Chat / message / blog facility.
- Can add multimedia content and hyperlinks.

(ii) One of:
- Tracking son / daughter's progress.
- Checking test results.
- Seeing what homework there is.

58. Social networks

(a) Any **two** from:
- Sharing photos.
- Online chat.
- Email.
- Reviews.

(b) Any **two** from:
- Could lead to a loss of privacy.
- Privacy settings change so he will have to stay up to date.
- People may impersonate others.

(c) Any **two** from:
- He can discuss with a lot of people at once in a coordinated way.
- Easy way to make new friends with similar interests.
- Easier to share files with a lot of people.
- He can know who is online at the same time and chat with them and other friends simultaneously.
- He can see updates on what other friends have done.
- He can add more information for a lot of people to see, for example blogs.

(d) The target audience for the two social networks is different: one is for work and one is social. Different features are useful to different target audiences. Joe's photography social network might include features specific to photographers such as a list of jobs or interesting photoshoot venues, whereas the purely social one might include more sophisticated timelines, status updates or fun features such as 'poke'.

59. User-generated reference sites

(a) One of:
- The feature that allows all users to add and edit the content in a simple web browser it will allow Anton share information with colleagues and they could add their ideas.
- Changes can be tracked to see who has made contributions.
- Hyperlinked pages and images can be added to share information with colleagues.

(b) Any **two** from:
- Wikis can be easily changed by users and kept up to date.

- People from different parts of the world can work together.
- Changes can be tracked.

(c) One of:
- Internet forums or message boards allow people to hold discussions by posting messages about a certain subject.
- Newsgroups, like message boards, are communities which discuss a particular topic.
- Reviews sites enable people to share their experiences of their purchase to help others make more informed decisions.

60. Social bookmarking sites

(a) Users add weblinks rather than content, then share these 'bookmarks' with others.

(b) (i) One of:
- Her friend will have selected each bookmark herself, and will have read and understood the content of the website she has chosen. Search engine results are often found by software programs which look for key words, so may not be as accurate.
- Her friend may have spotted weblinks that have not yet been 'noticed' by the search engines.
- People can rank the links so she can see how useful they are.

(ii) One of:
- The bookmarks may be out of date.
- They may not be exactly about the topic she is looking for.
- She must be careful not to use the actual content in her project without permissions.
- She must be careful not to be influenced too much by her friend's choices, as her ideas should be her own.

61. Creation of knowledge

The following points would be valid in answer to this question. Remember that the quality of your argument is important too.

The Internet has revolutionised the way knowledge is created.

Positives:
- Content can be published immediately all over the world.
- Information is constantly updated and can be developed by the audience.
- Everyone can publish their information and ideas without restriction.
- Content can be shared automatically, for example through news feeds.
- People can collaborate on projects across the globe.
- Tools such as spreadsheets and databases within online workspaces help to create ideas , model different situations and solve problems.
- Users, rather than editors, can decide what information is important, for example Digg users can 'bury' news that they deem unimportant or inappropriate.

- Information and knowledge can be made accessible to everyone through ICT. University students can take courses and communicate with their tutors online.

Negatives:

- Can be overwhelming as amount of information is so vast.
- No one checks or edits – validity? Bias? Accuracy? It is important to be able to select what is relevant to you and also which information comes from a valid source.
- Digital divide: people without technology are unable to contribute to, or benefit from, a principle source of information today.

62. Impact on working practices

(a) Any **two** from:

- It will save her money.
- Flexible.
- Increased productivity.
- Reduces pollution.

(b) Any **two** from:

- Less social contact.
- Easy to work for long hours with no break.
- Distractions at home.

(c) Any **two** from:

- It makes tools such as spreadsheets and databases more readily available which makes it easier to tackle questions, create ideas and help solve problems.
- It allows people to communicate, collaborate and share ideas on a global scale.
- It has made a huge amount of information available to everyone so it has made it easier to carry out research.

(d) Any **two** from:

- People can work together on the same documents online.
- Working as a group people can get more work done in less time.
- It makes it easy to share ideas and be more creative.
- It helps people to help each other to solve problems.

(e) Any **two** from:

- Video conference.
- VoIP.
- Email.
- Online chat.

63. Socialising and responsible use

(a) Any **two** from:

- Honouring copyright laws by not making unauthorised copies of files.
- Respecting other people's opinions and work.
- Thanking and acknowledging people.
- Not posting inappropriate images or videos.
- Logging off after use.
- Not sharing passwords.

- Respecting others' privacy.
- Not adding people as friends unless she knows them in real life.
- Using privacy settings.
- Never posting personal details which would give away where she lives or where she will be.

(b) The following points would be valid in answer to this question. Remember that the quality of your argument is important too.

Benefits:

- Grouping of individuals into specific groups to share opinions / reviews.
- Meet and communicate with people to gather and share first-hand information and experiences, such as cooking, sports and music.
- You can read profile pages of members and select online members with who you would like to be friends.
- Promotes diversity because you can connect with people from around the world and learn about new cultures / languages / learning new things.
- You can share experiences with others by posting photos and videos.
- Range of media to suit different needs, such as video cam, voice and chat.
- 24/7 access to friends / time is not a barrier.
- Find old friends and reconnect with them.
- Networking with people could help you find new interests / jobs.
- Removes barriers to communication because users have various ways of communicating regardless of disabilities, such as chat and webcam.

Drawbacks:

- People behave differently online.
- Online experience is not the same as face to face / gestures and context are not always obvious.
- People might not be who they say they are / cyberbullying / harassing / stalking / grooming has led to panic and fear.
- Lack of privacy and 'down-time'.
- Access to inappropriate / misleading content.

64. A global scale

The following points would be valid in answer to this question. Remember that the quality of your argument is important too.

Positives:

- Global online communities allow people to communicate and collaborate on a global scale.
- Vast number of ways to communicate globally, for example social networking, blogging, email, video conferencing, VoIP and so on.
- ICT has speeded up the process of globalisation (globalisation is the coming together of worldwide societies).
- It is now easy to make purchases from around the world 24 / 7 / 365, so different time zones and public holidays in different countries do not prevent sales being made.

- We can select and pay for goods from around the world without leaving our homes.
- Helped by ICT, many companies have now 'gone global' with offices and customers around the world.

Negatives:

- Location does not matter so much, so workers may be sourced from abroad where it is cheaper resulting in unemployment in the original country.
- Enormous transnational companies may put smaller companies out of business.
- Loss of culture and individualism as large global companies introduce popular trends from other countries.
- Potential loss of languages other than English because most global transactions use English.
- Digital divide – more difficult for countries without access to the latest technology to compete.
- Some countries now censor or control access to social networking and search engines to help them to repress opposition to the government.

Example answer

ICT has meant our ability to communicate with people across the globe has been speeded up and countries worldwide now work together, which is known as globalisation.

You can now communicate with friends and relatives all over the world using email, social networks and VoIP; they all make it easier to keep in touch. As a result, families who are apart can see each other so they feel more involved in daily life. It also makes people more aware of other cultures and makes it easy to make new friends in other countries which would not have been possible without ICT.

Furthermore, people across the world can also collaborate on projects easily using collaborative software, so distance is not as important. Indeed it could actually enhance work as different people add insights from other cultures and experiences. Distance from the office is no longer an issue as people can easily have virtual meetings, which also has the advantage of saving time and environmental resources in travelling.

Companies now have the chance to have customers and offices all around the world all working together easily. ICT makes it very easy for them to 'go global'.

As some companies are now known the world over, people in all countries may want to buy from them to be fashionable, losing individualism. Some countries without widespread access to ICT may be 'left out' and unable to compete commercially in this global market.

In some countries where the Internet is freely available, the government may actually restrict access to users. Sometimes this is for good reasons, to protect children or to filter out dangerous material, but sometimes it is simply blocked to repress alternative opinions.

In summary, the Internet has speeded up globalisation, which has many advantages for individuals and organisations, but there are negative impacts that must be considered and acted upon where possible.

Issues

65. Security issues

(a) **Hacking** is gaining unauthorised access to computers and data often using networks.

(b) Any **two** from:
- Physical threats, for example flooding and theft
- Bluejacking
- Phishing
- Viruses
- Unsecured wireless networks.

(c) (i) There are many risks to data on digital devices. Backing up data allows us to restore the data even if it is deleted or lost from the original device.

(ii) Any **two** from:
- Keep rooms locked.
- Use up-to-date antivirus software.
- Secure wireless networks using a password and encrypt data travelling over the network.
- Use firewalls, passwords and encrypt the information travelling across networks.
- Keep Bluetooth switched off when not in use.

(d) Any **two** from:
- Impersonal address.
- Banks never ask you to confirm your personal details in this way.
- The URL doesn't start with https.
- Misspelling of 'your'.
- Threat to account if instructions are not followed.

(e) This is an example of phishing where criminals try to pose as genuine companies to persuade you to give your personal details. This is a risk to RedRose because if they followed the instructions the criminal would be able to use the details to access their bank account or sell their information on.

66. Privacy issues

The following points would be valid in answer to this question. Remember that the quality of your argument is important too.

Covert data collection:

- Online companies gathering statistics about users' searches and browsing habits / actions for marketing purposes.
- Cookie installation and spyware.
- ISPs are able to view data that pass through them.
- Government / police looking at individuals' computers without a warrant (Big Brother concept).
- Identity theft.

Overt data collection:

- Filling out forms / buying goods. Users provide personal data knowingly without realising implications.
- Requirements for users to 'opt in' to gain access to services.
- Complicated 'opt out' methods.

Responsibilities of businesses to protect customers' data:

- Privacy policies which ought to cover, among other things, the website's use of cookies and other trackers.
- **Data Protection Act** – companies holding our data are required by law:
  - to keep it secure
  - not to ask for more data than necessary
  - not to keep data any longer than necessary
  - to keep data accurate and up to date
  - not to use data for any other purpose without our consent.

Example answer

Data is collected by organisations whenever we shop online. This is a potential privacy risk because if this data got into criminals' hands they could commit identity theft.

Data is collected in a variety of ways by online shops. Overt methods involve our filling out forms containing personal details necessary when actually buying goods. Slightly less obvious ways are when users are required to opt-in and share data in order to gain access to information or free content. Some less reputable companies may make opt out methods complex to dissuade customers from opting out, or rely on users accepting complex terms without actually reading them.

Other data may be gathered without the user actually being aware of it. Online companies gather statistics about users' searches and browsing habits for marketing purposes. Cookies hold personal information about user preferences. This data can be useful to users because it allows them to receive tailored content and adverts about products that are more relevant to them. However, some people think that this use of data is an invasion of their privacy and do not appreciate a computer telling them what to buy. ISPs are able to view all data that passes through them and the police are allowed to look at individuals' computers and ISP data without a warrant.

As a result, businesses have a responsibility to protect customers' data. Reputable companies will have a privacy policy which will cover how the website uses cookies and other trackers. According to the Data Protection Act, companies holding our data are required by law to keep it secure and not to use it for any other purpose without our consent. Third party payment processors also help keep our payment data safe by preventing it from being passed on to sellers.

Shopping online involves giving out personal details which is always a privacy risk. It is important to be careful to only shop with reputable firms and also careful not to give out information unless necessary.

67. Monitoring movements and communications

(a) Geotagging information gives an exact location. 'Friends' in social networks are not necessarily people who you have met face to face. Location information could be passed to enemies who could use this information to launch an attack very accurately.

(b) The following points would be valid in answer to this question. Remember that the quality of your argument is important too.

Tracking movement and communication helps us by:

- Mobile phone companies can track our position and software is available to track location of friends using their phones. If someone goes missing with their phone, police or family / friends can locate them.
- It is convenient – friends who agree to share this information can always know where the others are if, for example, they need them urgently.
- Police can use mobile phone data to track down criminals.
- Government access to all phone and Internet records can help prevent serious crime such as terrorism.
- The use of credit / debit cards allows the banks to know when, where and how much money you spend. This enables them to note when spending patterns change and to verify with you that your card is not being used fraudulently.
- Geotagging on social networking sites can add a whole new level of information which can be useful for people planning visits or tracking their friends' travels.
- The IP address of your computer provides clues to search engines and social networking sites about your geographical location. This enables them to tailor results and information to your area, making it more relevant and convenient.
- Passports are now scanned when going in and out of different countries. This enables the police to track the movement of criminals.
- Helping us find our way through using GPS on satellite navigation devices.
- Local services can be found.
- Augmented reality can be used to play games or display localised content to users.

Potential objections:

- Monitoring software which tracks the position of mobile phones can be set up without the phone owner's knowledge and so he or she can be tracked unknowingly. However, this is about keeping personal items safe, rather than anything to do with technology – if someone had access to someone's purse / wallet they would similarly have very personal details.
- Big Brother fears from police / government on tracking everything we do. But this only becomes an issue if we have something to hide and so this should promote an honest society. This also applies to passport monitoring.
- Data from banks about spending patterns could get into the wrong hands. However, banks' security and privacy procedures are very good and this is highly unlikely.
- Geotagging could provide a security risk as people can actually find the people they meet online. But geotagging is no different from other personal information, so people should just be aware of the risk and be careful with how they share it – as with any other personal information. But this should not prevent people from using a very useful feature.

Example answer

Tracking movement and communication using technology is extremely useful to our everyday lives.

Firstly, it can help with security and safety. For example, mobile phone companies can track our position and software is available to track where our friends are using their phones and if someone goes missing with their phone, police or family or friends can locate them. Furthermore, the police can use mobile phone data to track down criminals, and the government has access to all phone and Internet records to help them prevent serious crime such as terrorism. At borders, passports are now scanned, which enables criminals' movements to be tracked.

Although some people argue that there are privacy issues with tracking devices and software and feel as though their civil liberties are being reduced, it could be argued that this only becomes an issue if we have something to hide and actually, it promotes an honest society.

The use of credit / debit cards allows banks to know when, where and how much money people spend. This enables them to note when spending patterns change and to verify with them that cards are not being used fraudulently. Sometimes it is thought that data from banks about spending patterns could get into the wrong hands. However, banks argue that their security and privacy procedures are very good and this is highly unlikely.

It is also very convenient – friends who agree to sharing this information can always know where the others are if, for example, they need them urgently. Geotagging on social networking sites can add a whole new level of information which can be useful for people planning visits or tracking their friends' travels.

Geotagging could produce a security risk because people can actually find the people they meet online. But geotagging is no different from other personal information, so people should just be aware of the risk and be careful with how they share it – as with any other personal information.

The IP address of your computer provides clues to search engines and social networking sites about your geographical location. This enables them to tailor results and information to your area, making it more relevant and convenient. In addition, augmented reality can be used to play games or display localised content to users. GPS on satellite navigation devices can help us find our way and local services can be found.

In summary, as with any technology, there are certain risks. But these should not be allowed to outweigh the benefit of the huge advantages tracking technology has to offer.

68. Health and safety

(a) Any **two** from:

- Repetitive strain injuries can develop from doing the same thing / movement again and again.
- ICT can contribute to obesity due to inactivity. Time is also spent using technology rather than completing work or school work.
- People can always access their work, even on holiday or in the evening, so can become ill or stressed as they feel they are unable to stop working.

- Joint pain can result from sitting incorrectly for a long time.
- Eye strains can be caused by staring at a screen for a long time.
- It may be possible that the radio waves from mobile phones and base stations may affect health.
- Accidents can be caused by people using mobile phones whilst driving.
- Hand-held GPS devices have resulted in accidents for mountain walkers.

(b) 1 Exercises at home using games such as the Wii can improve physical fitness.

2 Accurate health and fitness monitoring.

(c) Using digital devices in your hand whilst driving is illegal and dangerous. Trying to steer and operate a device such as a phone can distract you from driving and make you look away from the road so that you do not see hazards ahead as quickly, for example children in the road. Hands-free devices help to minimise this risk.

69. The impact of networks

The following points would be valid in answer to this question. Remember that the quality of your argument is important too.

Work:

- Teleworking (working from home).
- Work easily with people all over world.
- Location of office less important.
- Office / home networks allow users to share resources and have access to a range of resources.
- Research for projects online.

Shopping:

- Rapid access.
- Round-the-clock availability.
- No need to leave house.
- Research purchases more easily.

Communication:

- Socialising with people all around the world, 24/7.
- Over use of social networking sites.
- Rapid spread of news.

Creativity:

- Crowd sourcing (people are collecting news and contributing content to websites).
- People become content generators for websites, for example YouTube, Wikipedia and Udraw.

Digital divide:

- Those that do not have access to networks are not able to access some information, goods and services.
- This is leading to a widening of the gap between the groups of people, both within and between countries.

70. Legislation relating to the use of ICT

(a) **A** Planting viruses

(b) One of:

- The Data Protection Act (DPA) protects us against misuse of our personal data which may be held by a range of organisations, for example shops, schools and government. These organisations must ensure that our personal data is collected for real purposes and fairly, not kept longer than necessary, kept secure and not transferred outside of Europe.

- The Copyright, Designs and Patents Act makes it a criminal offence to copy or steal media or other people's work or ideas. Many people do not realise that it is illegal to copy material in this way even if you are not selling it on, unless you have a special licence or permission from the copyright holder. Similarly it is illegal to use software on more computers than you have licences for, and also to copy images, text and music from websites without the copyright owner's permission.

- The Digital Economy Act stops people illegally downloading media. Internet Service Providers (ISPs) can collect data about repeat offenders. If offenders continue downloading then their Internet access can be slowed or suspended.

71. Unequal access to ICT

(a) Any **two** from:

- James will have fewer IT skills so less likely to get a well-paid job.

- James will have less access to online information which means, for example, he cannot do online training to help him get a better job.

- No access to online goods and services so cannot compare deals / features as easily.

- Unable to take calls when out and about, so could miss out on job opportunities and the social convenience and safety a mobile phone offers.

- Less social interaction online so could feel 'left out' if friends are online.

(b) The following points would be valid in answer to this question. Remember that the quality of your argument is important too.

Economic impact:

- More limited skills development and understanding of the use of technology.

- Limited awareness / skills can impact on jobs.

- More difficult to access banking and other online services.

- Goods cost more – often cheaper to buy goods / services online.

- Less choice – wider range of options re goods / services if can access easily online.

- The Internet has led to a rise in e-commerce and globalisation. Countries without good access to ICT are not developing as fast as those who do.

Social impact:

- Digital exclusion.

- Poorer online communication (less immediate) access to email / other comms (also applies to mobile phones and so on not just broadband). Especially important with people abroad as much more difficult to contact them.

- Exclusion – opportunity to link into social networking / developing friendship / common interest groups, especially globally as technology is the main way of contact.

- Access to 'now' society – immediate contact / access to news.

Educational impact:

- Poorer access to information / many educational resources now freely available on line especially through VLEs.

- Online courses.

- No access to online training – need to access community resources – need to leave home to do this.

- More limited opportunity for development of skills – ICT and other functional skills.

Cultural impact:

- Access to resources such as:
  - music – MP3/4 players / downloads / streaming
  - video on demand
  - TV BBC iPlayer and similar.

- Some religious groups restrict their members access to digital technology.

- People may be stereotyped by gender, for example boys and men may be given more access to, and education in, technology than girls and women.

- Children with access to technology may play on games consoles rather than playing outside.

72. Safe and responsible practice

(a) Any **two** from:

- It is unhealthy to sit at a desk all day without a break because he could suffer from eye strain, RSI and so on.

- He could spill his drink on his computer which could result in an electric shock.

- Harmful bacteria can live on a keyboard – if he eats while he is typing, he is unable to wash his hands and this could make him ill.

(b) Any **two** from:

- He could use ergonomic equipment, for example keyboards and chairs.

- He should take breaks or change position regularly.

- He could receive training to use the digital devices effectively.

(c) Any **two** from:

- They could have a fault which causes them to overheat.

- They could not be properly ventilated which causes them to overheat.

- Extension sockets could be overloaded, causing a fire.

(d) Any **two** from:

- Use of technology is essential in modern world – need to develop skills to be successful and socialise effectively.

- Technology develops hand–eye co-ordination which is essential in everyday life.
- Technology use is linked to improved reading skills which is important in everyday life where we are constantly surrounded by written communication.
- Technology can save time e.g. shopping online rather than going to supermarket which can give more time for relaxation.
- Friendships can be built / maintained online as it is easier to contact people more frequently using technology e.g. Skype.
- Access to information about health and well-being online can make Henry more aware of risks and precautions.
- Technology can be used to encourage exercising e.g. Wii Fit, which is directly related to health.
- Health and fitness can be monitored using technology, which encourages a healthy pace and may highlight risks.
- Technology can be used to track Henry's location and to communicate while he's out and about, which can help keep him in contact with others, keeping him safe.

73. Sustainability issues

(a) Any **two** from:
- You can keep using the device for as long as possible before replacing it.
- You can use your devices responsibly by switching them off when not in use.
- You could choose devices which are energy efficient.
- You can use a renewable power source, for example solar energy.

(b) The following points would be valid in answer to this question. Remember that the quality of your argument is important too.

Environmental benefits of ICT:
- Teleworking reduces the need to commute.
- Digital versions of traditional paper items, for example newspapers, books reduces the need for paper.
- Computers in card improve fuel economy.
- Emails/texts have a smaller carbon footprint than letters, especially globally.
- Online shopping reduces the need to drive to the shops, saving petrol.

Sustainability issues of ICT:

E-waste
- Old computer equipment ends up as electronic waste (e-waste) that goes to landfill sites.
- More developed countries are now sending e-waste to less developed countries.

Pollution
- Toxic substances from e-waste can get into the soil and water supplies.
- All digital devices use electricity. Large computers need even more electricity to keep them cool.

The traditional generation of electricity produces greenhouses gases that can cause global warming.

Finite resources
- Some of the elements used to create digital devices are in short supply so will run out one day.
- Electricity often comes from non-renewable resources such as coal and oil (fossil fuels), which will also run out in future.

Ways to improve sustainability of ICT:

Recycle
- Recycle or reuse the digital devices.
- Donate unwanted digital devices to organizations who provide computers to poorer countries.
- Companies will now buy your unwanted digital devices from you so they are reused.
- Some companies are now taking apart electronic waste and selling the parts.

Reduce your use
- Use digital devices for as long as possible before replacing (reduce your use).
- Switch off digital devices when they are not in use and when batteries are charged.
- Use devices that have a sleep mode when not in use.

Renewable energy
- Companies who run large servers are now locating to locations with cool climates and cheap sustainable electricity (for example Iceland which has cool water for cooling and hydroelectric power).
- Technology companies are starting to offer solar-powered devices.

Practice exam paper

1 (a) (i) Camera C

(ii) Camera D

(iii) Camera B

(iv) Camera B

(b) Any **two** from:

- A digital camera might have an optical zoom.
- A digital camera is likely to have a larger sensor area.
- Flash on a camera is far better than the LED lights on a smartphone.
- Digital cameras can shoot more images per second.
- Can save in more formats on a digital camera e.g. RAW.
- On a digital camera you can make more adjustments e.g. manually change the shutter speed or aperture.

(c) (i) The geographical coordinates.

OR

Longitude, latitude, elevation.

(ii) She will know exactly where she took the picture.

OR

Her friends will be able to use Google Maps / Earth to see exactly where she is.

(iii) People she does not know will be able to find out her location / which may put her in danger from stalkers.

(d) Any **two** from:

- She can set the album as 'private'.
- She can state who can view the album and send a notifying email.
- She can set further access rights e.g. who can edit or make comments.

2 (a) Two benefits to Millie – any **two** from:

- Greater choice.
- Can shop around and compare prices.
- Can shop 24/7.
- Can read other people's reviews / opinions before buying.
- Has the right to return goods within seven days for any reason.

(b) One drawback to Millie – **one** of:

- Can't try the camera / may have to send it back.
- Has to wait for it to be delivered.
- Actual product might be different from online presentation and description.
- Need to have credit/debit card / third party payment account / can't pay by cash.
- May have to pay a delivery charge.
- Security risk e.g. identity theft.

(c) Any **two** from:

- Save money on rent / rates / lighting, etc.
- Don't have to pay shop staff.
- Don't have to buy in stock for customers to see / can get products when they are ordered.
- Can sell world-wide.
- Can sell 24/7/365 / across time zones.

(d) (i) Any **two** from:

- Data must be held securely.
- Data must be used only for the purpose for which it was collected.
- Data must be accurate.
- Data must be up to date.
- Personal data shall not be transferred to a country or territory outside the European Economic Area unless that country or territory ensures an adequate level of protection for the rights and freedoms of data subjects in relation to the processing of personal data.
- Data collected should be adequate and relevant and not excessive in relation to the purpose for which it is collected.
- The Data Subject has the right to see the data and ask for it to be amended.

(ii) C The Data Protection Act

(iii) D Privacy Policy

(e) 1 The URL should change to https://.

2 The padlock icon (or similar indicator) should appear on the address bar and if double-clicked should show the security certificate.

(f) (i) One of:

- It saves her having to type her password in again.
- Her view of the website is personalised.
- She can receive customised recommendations based on her shopping preferences.

(ii) Any **two** from:

- To free up storage space on her computer.
- To stop unsolicited personalised adverts.
- To stop organisations getting hold of her personal information/ browsing habits.
- To stop people finding out about her personal information / browsing habits (shared computer).

3 (a) (i) D Convergence

(ii) Any **two** from:

- Sending emails.
- Browsing Internet.
- Listening to music / watching videos / looking at stored photographs.
- Sat nav.
- Using apps (applications) e.g. compass, torch, word processing, etc.
- Playing games.

(iii) **One** of:

- Games console – stream films / online chat on Internet / video calls.
- Sat nav – store images / Bluetooth links to mobile phones so they can be used for hands free calls.
- Digital camera – Wi-Fi to allow users to upload images directly without using a computer.

(b) (i) **C** Roaming

(ii) **A** SMS

(c) (i) **One** of:

- She could transfer them wirelessly by using Bluetooth.
- She could take the flash memory card out of the camera and insert it into her laptop.
- She could transfer them using a wired connection by using a USB cable.

(ii) **One** of:

- Blu-ray drive.
- Memory stick / card / USB drive.
- External hard drive.
- Personal media player.

(iii) Any **two** from:

- Data will not be lost if she loses her digital devices.
- She does not have to carry USB drives / memory sticks, etc. around with her.
- She can allow others to access it remotely.
- Data is safe if her devices are damaged.

(d) (i) Pair / connect / link the devices / using Wi-Fi.

OR

Set up the phone as a router / hotspot / and use Wi-Fi.

(ii) **One** of:

- Set up an access code / password / PIN.
- Block unknown devices (MAC filtering).
- Hide SSID.
- Make sure other devices are not within range.

(iii) As more devices use the connection, the available bandwidth is reduced / less / divided.

4 (a) (i) A way of linking / connecting people using their personal information

OR

A way of creating / maintaining an online community

(ii) Any **two** from:

- She can communicate with lots of friends at the same time.
- The friends don't have to be available at the time – they can read Millie's messages later.
- There is a record of the communication.

- If there is a free Wi-Fi hotspot available, it will be cheaper than making voice calls for which Millie will have to pay roaming charges.

(iii) Any **two** from:

- Risk of identity theft.
- Makes them vulnerable to predators / cyber bullying.
- Loss of privacy.

(b) (i) **B** VoIP

(ii) 1 Microphone

2 Speakers

(c) (i) The messages remain on the mail server. They are not downloaded to her local computer.

(ii) **One** of:

- More storage space on her local computer.
- She can access them from any other computer / device.

(d) (i) **C** The Copyright Act

(ii) Explanation to include:

Adds metadata / key words to the post which allows it to be categorised / indexed which makes it easier to search for and view other work by this author.

(e) The following points would be valid in an answer to this question. Remember that the quality of your argument is important too.

- Gives more people a voice / more people can publish.
- More freedom of speech / less censorship.
- People can self-publish using blogs, wikis, personal websites, etc.
- More people can make money from publishing their work.
- People can more easily build a world-wide following for their work.
- Readers can share articles with networks of friends.
- Stories / information popularised by public, not editors.
- Work can quickly find a large audience – go 'viral'.
- Competition drives traditional publishers to innovate with their provision of online content.
- e-democracy – information is made available to/from politically 'sensitive' areas.
- As more is published it is harder to sift through all the material to find 'quality' work.
- Harder to check if copyright is being infringed.

Really good answers will discuss a range of positive and negative impacts relevant to the publishing of work on the Internet. The impacts discussed will be factually accurate and clearly justified. The answer will be focused and organised and will include appropriate specialist terms. Spelling punctuation and the rules of grammar will be used accurately.

5 (a) (i) Any **three** points from:
- They can hand in any work they have been set to do while they're away.
- They can view their marked homework and receive feedback.
- They can answer their teacher's or friends' questions about the places they are visiting on their trip.
- They can post details of their trip and upload photographs.

(ii) Any **two** from:
- She can add pictures.
- She can add text.
- She can add web links.
- She can add news feeds.

(b) (i) **C** The digital divide

(ii) Any **two** from:
- They may not be able to afford digital devices / Internet connection.
- They may live in an area / country where there is poor infrastructure / access to Internet.
- They may have weak literacy skills.
- They may have a disability.

(iii) Any **four** points from:
- May affect their employment chances.
- Poorer access to goods and services.
- Less able to take advantage of e-commerce and globalisation.
- Cannot research material for education.
- Cannot take advantage of educational VLEs.
- Cannot take advantage of online courses.
- Cannot communicate using emails, instant messaging, use forums, etc.
- Cannot take advantage of entertainment possibilities e.g. streaming video, TV on demand.

(c) The following points would be valid in an answer to this question. Remember that the quality of your argument is important too.

Negative impacts of increased use on environment:

Production
- Large amounts of fossil fuels are used to generate the electricity to make computers – up to ten times the weight of the computer.
- Large number of toxic chemicals used in the production of digital devices.
- Harmful chemicals such as lead and mercury can be released into the environment if they are not properly disposed of (economic implications of safe disposal).

Use
- Large amount of energy – generated by fossil fuels – is used to run digital devices.
- Pollution is produced in the process / toxic and carbon dioxide emissions.

Disposal
- Plastics used in the hardware e.g. keyboard cannot be recycled – disposed of in landfill sites.
- Many discarded computers (e-waste) are shipped to third world countries where they cause pollution and health risks.
- Positive impact of increased use on environment:
- Use in monitoring the environment for harmful emissions, etc.
- Control systems for managing the environment.
- Allow scientists to build complex models of the environment / climate change.
- Shopping online causes less pollution than visiting shops.
- Paying bills etc. online causes less pollution e.g. no paper used, no delivery.
- Some sat navs and apps let you plan the route which causes the least pollution.

Improving sustainability:
- Re-use old equipment / donate to charities for others to use.
- Educate people to switch off when not using / recycle.
- Make manufacturers pay a contribution to pollution and recycling costs.

Really good answers will discuss a range of positive and negative impacts relevant to the effects of digital equipment on the environment. The impacts discussed will be factually accurate and clearly justified. The answer will be focused and organised and will include appropriate specialist terms. Spelling punctuation and the rules of grammar will be used accurately.

Your own notes

Your own notes

Your own notes

Your own notes

Your own notes

Published by Pearson Education Limited, Edinburgh Gate, Harlow, Essex, CM20 2JE.

www.pearsonschoolsandfecolleges.co.uk

Copies of official specifications for all Edexcel qualifications may be found on the Edexcel website:
www.edexcel.com

Text and original illustrations © Pearson Education Limited 2012
Edited and produced by Wearset, Boldon, Tyne and Wear
Illustrated and typeset by HL Studios, Witney, Oxfordshire
Cover illustration by Miriam Sturdee

The rights of Nicola Hughes and David Waller to be identified as authors of this work have been asserted
by them in accordance with the Copyright, Designs and Patents Act 1988.

First published 2012

16 15 14 13 12

10 9 8 7 6 5 4 3 2 1

British Library Cataloguing in Publication Data
A catalogue record for this book is available from the British Library

ISBN 978 1 446 90389 6

Printed in Slovakia by Neografia

Acknowledgements

The author and publisher would like to thank the following individuals and organisations for permission
to reproduce photographs:

(Key: b-bottom; c-centre; l-left; r-right; t-top)

Alamy Images: Angela Hampton Picture Library 74, Blend Images 39, Inspirestock Inc. 44; **Getty
Images:** Blend Images 51; **Pearson Education Ltd:** Jon Barlow 47; **Science Photo Library Ltd:**
AJ Photo 45; **Shutterstock.com:** Ilji Mašik 46; **SuperStock:** SOMOS 53, 54

Every effort has been made to contact copyright holders of material reproduced in this book. Any
omissions will be rectified in subsequent printings if notice is given to the publishers.

In the writing of this book, no Edexcel examiners authored sections relevant to examination papers for
which they have responsibility.